Leonardo da Vinci

...d Freud was born on 6 May 1856 in the village of Freiberg, Moravia,
...rt of the Czech Republic, into a Jewish merchant family. When he was
...ars old his family moved to Vienna, where Freud remained until the
...vasion and occupation in 1938.

...d began his education in 1873 at the University of Vienna at the age
...enteen. He was initially interested in law, then zoology and later
...ogy. As a student he also admired his philosophy tutor Franz
Bre... no, who investigated but later rejected the possibility of an
unco... cious mind. He also read Nietzsche, writing that he hoped to find in
...che's works 'the words for much that remains mute in me'.

...uing the study of neurology he travelled to Paris in 1885 to work with
...Martin Charcot, who was leading the study of hysteria and had a close
...terest in hypnosis. Freud found both areas of study extremely interesting
...der Charcot's direction turned from medicine to the emerging field of
...ology. In 1886, Freud returned from Paris to Vienna, where he opened
...ate practice specializing in nervous and brain disorders. That same
y... ...e married Martha Bernays, with whom he had six children in the span
...e years.

...ally using hypnosis with his patients, Freud found that a more effective
...n of symptom relief could be achieved, without recourse to hypnosis, by
...uraging patients to talk freely about whatever ideas or memories occurred
...m – a method which he called 'free association'. Freud also found that a
T...t's dreams could be fruitfully analyzed to reveal unconscious material
a further pe... ...ssion at the root of symptom formation. By 1896 Freud
the above numb... ...term 'psychoanalysis' to r...

Enquiries: ...

www.rotherh...

In 1902, Freud was appointed associate professor at the University of Vienna. The Wednesday Psychological Society was born, where Freud and his followers met to discuss their work, marking the beginnings of the psychoanalytic movement. In 1906 Freud began correspondence with Carl Jung, though they later fell out over Jung's commitment to spirituality and occultism, which Freud regarded as unscientific.

During the First World War, Freud had three sons fighting in combat. Initially a patriot and generally supportive of the German war effort he grew increasingly disillusioned by the conflict. Appalled by human destructiveness on such a huge scale, several of Freud's concepts concerning competing life and death drives, later formalized in *Beyond the Pleasure Principle* (1920) and *Civilization and Its Discontents* (1930), came together in this period.

In 1938 Ernest Jones, the then president of the International Psychoanalytic Association, flew into Vienna determined to get Freud to flee the emerging Nazi threat and seek exile in Britain. Freud arrived in London in June 1938, where he continued to see patients and worked on his final books, *Moses and Monotheism* (1938) and the uncompleted *Outline of Psychoanalysis*, which was published posthumously. Four of Freud's five sisters died in concentration camps. Freud's brother, Alexander, escaped with his family to Switzerland, subsequently emigrating to Canada. Freud's sons Oliver, a civil engineer, and Ernst Ludwig, an architect, lived and worked in Berlin until Hitler came to power, after which they fled with their families to France and London respectively.

By 1939 Freud's mouth cancer, brought on by his regular cigar-smoking, was declared inoperable. He died in London of a morphine overdose in September 1939.

Maria Walsh is a Senior Lecturer in Art History and Theory at Chelsea College of Art & Design. She has contributed chapters to a number of books on the topic of film spectatorship, affect, and embodiment, including *Screen/Space: The Projected Image in Contemporary Art*, 2011. Her monograph *Art and Psychoanalysis* was published by I.B. Tauris in 2012. She is a regular contributor to *Art Monthly* and is a member of the AHRC Peer Review College.

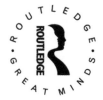

Sigmund
Freud

Leonardo da Vinci

A memory of his childhood

Translated by Alan Dyson

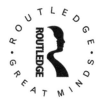 London and New York

First published 1910 by Deuticke

English edition with Preface by Ernest Jones first published in the United Kingdom 1922 by Kegan Paul
This translation first published 1957
by Routledge and Kegan Paul as part of the International Library of Psychology

First published in Routledge Classics 2001
This edition published in Routledge Great Minds 2014
2 Park Square, Milton Park, Abingdon, Oxon, OX14 4RN

Routledge is an imprint of the Taylor & Francis Group, an informa business

© 1957 The Institute of Psycho-Analysis and Anna Richards

© 2014 foreword, Maria Walsh

Typeset in Joanna by RefineCatch Limited, Bungay, Suffolk
Printed by Bell and Bain Ltd, Glasgow

British Library Cataloguing in Publication Data
A catalogue record for this book is available from the British Library

ISBN: 978–0–415–85467–2

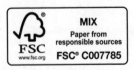

Contents

Contents

FOREWORD TO THE ROUTLEDGE GREAT MINDS EDITION

A classic is a book that is returned to. It has the capacity to generate new interpretations over time. Freud's *Leonardo da Vinci: A Memoir of his Childhood* is one such book. By turns either absolutely dismissed or completely accepted,[1] how might it speak to us today? First published in 1910 and translated into English in 1916, it is, like most of Freud's texts, a circuitous read as it oscillates between concepts of sublimation and repression, memory and fantasy, and maternal and paternal identification, all in relation to Leonardo's own fluctuation between artistic activity and scientific research. Ostensibly a psychobiography or a 'pathography' of Leonardo, using a select number of his paintings and drawings as material evidence of his psyche along with other biographies to furnish details of his life, the text is fascinating on many counts. In it, we find Freud's first forays into his theories of narcissism, which he would later develop into the paper 'On Narcissism: An Introduction' (1914); Freud's main account of male homosexuality, which is here developed further from the earlier paper 'Three Essays on Sexuality' (1905); and, interestingly, Freud's own identification with his subject, a feature often foreclosed in traditional biographical writing. Freud's desire to establish psychoanalysis as a science leads him to prioritise science as the highest form of sublimation in *Leonardo da Vinci* and to consider it in terms of a paternal narrative of rivalry, rather than to explore the narcissistic field of the maternal that he intuits in Leonardo's painting. It is this latter trajectory that speaks more to us today as we look for alignments between psychoanalysis and art in terms of how it elaborates affect, memory, and the imaginary rather than any claim to scientific truth.

Freud's analysis of Leonardo is usually dismissed because of its reliance on a mistranslation of a memory recounted in Leonardo's scientific notebooks. Examining the dynamics of flight, Leonardo recalls 'as one of my very earliest memories that while I was in my cradle a vulture [kite] came down to me, and opened my mouth with its tail, and struck me many times with its tail against [within] my lips' (30). In the German translations that Freud was working from, the Italian *nibbio* was translated as vulture rather than kite. While for the 'ancients' such childhood fables in which animals land on the mouths of great men refer to the motif of inspiration,[2] for Freud, whose Enlightenment project has no truck with such superstitions, this 'memory' is a fable about the child's initiation into sexuality. He interprets Leonardo's memory as a seduction fantasy, the oral nature of the bird's tail in his mouth representing his mother's passionate kisses, the overwhelming pleasure of which are later elaborated into the derivation of sexual pleasure from *fellatio*, which Freud associates with femininity and homosexuality. Freud categorized Leonardo's homosexuality as being the result of an attachment to an all-powerful maternal figure with whom Leonardo identifies and, in taking her place in his imagination, so chooses his love objects, i.e. boys, in terms of their similarity to himself. In 'On Narcissism', Freud would later claim that this kind of narcissistic structure is key to artistic activity, but in *Leonardo da*

Vinci he does not pursue this connection, instead focussing on how details of Leonardo's biography might have led to his tendency to leave his works unfinished.

According to psychoanalyst Jean Laplanche, who has rescued Freud's seduction theory from discredit as a denial of sexual abuse, the work of art, as too the work of memory, is a symbolic working through of early affects and sensations which we did not have the means to understand at the time we received them— perhaps the passionate kisses of a mother. These enigmatic messages, which relate to such fundamental questions as 'what does the other want of me?', 'where did I come from?' or 'where do babies come from?' drive the early sexual researches of the child which are later elaborated into either neurotic symptoms or non-neurotic sublimations.[3] The paradox in *Leonardo da Vinci* is that while, on the one hand, Freud reduces Leonardo's art to being a compensatory object for a lost 'blissful union between mother and child', he also provides the basis of an approach to sublimation that severs this link between sublimation and repression. Unfortunately, because Freud never went on to write a paper on sublimation,[4] a misguided notion of sublimation persists in the popular imagination, in which the work of art is thought to be the release of frustrated sexuality, the result of a drive whose aim has been diverted from sexual ends towards cultural ones. However, in *Leonardo da Vinci*, Freud gives us three scenarios of sublimation. And while all three stem from the earliest sexual researches of the child into questions concerning origins, they have different outcomes.

Unable to answer these questions due to sexual immaturity, the child, Freud says, abandons his early investigations but 'the instinct for research has three distinct possible vicissitudes open to it' (27). In the first of these, research, along with sexuality, is inhibited. In this scenario, intellectual activity is stymied, the individual's development of a neurotic symptom becoming the means by which s/he remains attached to these now repressed questions. In the second vicissitude, the suppressed sexual activities of research re-emerge from the unconscious and reattach themselves to intellectual activity which takes on 'the pleasure and anxiety that belong to sexual processes proper', thereby the individual becomes subject to obsessive and compulsive brooding (27). But, in the third vicissitude of the instinct, 'the libido evades the fate of repression by being sublimated from the very beginning into curiosity and by becoming attached to the powerful instinct for research as a reinforcement. Here [. . .] there is no attachment to the original complexes of infantile sexual research, and the instinct can operate freely in the service of intellectual interest' (28). This third vicissitude allows us to consider sublimation as a process that moves us away from fixation on a lost or repressed object, often in psychoanalysis considered to be the mother's body, and towards the mobility and freedom of research. This gives rise to a number of contradictions in Freud's text.

In the first part of the text, Freud offers Leonardo as an example of the third type of sublimation but he only claims this in relation to his scientific curiosity not in relation to his artistic activity, concluding that: 'His later scientific research with all its boldness and independence, presupposed the existence of infantile sexual researches *uninhibited by his father*, and was a prolongation of them with the sexual element excluded' (80; emphasis added). (Leonardo is thought to have spent the early years of his life alone with his mother before moving at around five years of age to his father's house.) However, by the end of the text, Freud places Leonardo 'close to the type of neurotic that we describe as "obsessional"; and we may compare his researches to the "obsessive brooding" of neurotics' (90). Why this change of heart?

For Freud, the father introduces the law, i.e. the threat of castration, which is necessary to break up the maternal dyad and propel the boy child towards a resolution of the oedipal complex.

Without this prohibition of his early attachment and identification with the mother, the individual is subject to perversion or psychosis. While Leonardo's homosexuality is categorised by Freud as perversion, he is at pains to explain Leonardo's extraordinary capacity for sublimation as well as his 'symptom', according to Vasari, of leaving his works unfinished. However questionable Freud's theory of homosexuality may be, he cannot entertain the possibility that Leonardo's capacity for sublimation could be derived from his narcissistic identification with a seductive phallic mother, as this would situate sublimation in relation to a passive, feminine aim. Instead, the essay goes on to account for Leonardo's achievements in scientific research in relation to a 'period of masculine creative power' (91) and the later identifications that Leonardo made with men such as his biological father, a prosperous notary, and his patron, the duke Ludovico Moro. Freud now locates the third vicissitude of the instinct in which sublimation and repression are delinked to a paternal narrative of identification and rivalry, deftly moving the reader away from the maternal dyadic universe in which this vicissitude initially originated. As Lacanian psychoanalyst Darian Leader states: 'Freud links sublimation to the recognition of the abstract dimension of paternity over the physicality of the relation to the mother'.[5] Leonardo's failure then is that he is not scientific enough, as his research still retains a strong connection to the physical nature of the human body. This 'failure' is Leonardo's success as an artist.

Freud believed that the creative artist feels like a father towards his works, which leads him to assert that Leonardo treated his paintings as his father treated him: by abandoning them or not being interested in finishing them. As Freud states, Leonardo's scientific research was first taken on to serve his art but later becomes the dominant force in his life, leading him to neglect his painting. His interest in painting is renewed on meeting Mona Lisa Del Giacondo who, Freud claims, reawakened the memory of his mother's smile. A fruitful period of painting ensued, the enigmatic smile of the infamous Mona Lisa 1503–6 being repeated in The Virgin and Child with St. Anne, 1508 and in subsequent portraits of androgynous young men, St. John the Baptist and Bacchus. This smile also occurs in the cartoon The Virgin and Child with St. Anne and the Infant Saint John the Baptist, and, although there is no agreement as to whether this was work executed c. 1499–1500 or c. 1506–8, Freud prefers the latter date as it corroborates his theory: it is only after having met Mona Lisa that he can now give his mother the smile she never had in life, thereby situating the work of art as a substitution and/or compensation.

Although Freud admits at the end of the text to failing to understand how 'artistic activity derives from the primal instincts of the mind' (91), he does not hesitate to retreat to the common view that Leonardo's art is an outlet for sexual desire for his mother and for boys like himself to whom he directs his love in his identification with her. Freud fails to follow through on his more radical theory of sublimation, which would keep the artist in an uninhibited process of sublimating rather than neurotic fixation. Here it is Leonardo's attachment to the body that drives him to find new objects of narcissistic identification, which include his interest in the mechanisms of flight. We can see this in his attitude to nature in his Treatise on Painting:

> if you cast your glance on any walls dirty with such stains or walls made up of rock formations of different types. If you have to invent some scenes, you will be able to discover them there in diverse forms, in diverse landscapes, adorned with mountains, rivers, rocks, trees, extensive plains, valleys, and hills. You can even see different battle scenes and movements made up of unusual figures, faces with strange expressions, and myriad things which you can transform into a complete and proper form constituting part of similar walls and rocks.

This passage exemplifies a way of relating to things in terms of affinity rather than objective distance. It shows the artist less as the father of his works than as someone who is captivated by the infinite possibilities of the imagination, the natural world providing the means of uninhibited identifications between self and other. Similarly, Leonardo's replication of smiles can be seen as repeating the excitations of maternal seduction rather than restoring a lost universe that may have never existed.[6] Leonardo's uninhibited curiosity allows him to transpose nature's enigmas into the joy of painting; a propensity not permitted Freud the scientist, but perhaps countenanced by Freud the literary critic for whom this essay remained his favourite composition.

MARIA WALSH
April 2013

Notes

1 The art historian Meyer Schapiro debunked its lack of historical accuracy in his 'Leonardo and Freud: An Art-Historical Study', *Journal of the History of Ideas*, Vol. 17, No. 2 (Apr., 1956), pp. 147–78. Psychoanalyst Julia Kristeva adheres strictly to Freud's interpretation in her 1980 book, *Desire in Language: A Semiotic Approach to Literature and Art*, Basil Blackwell.

2 See Schapiro, pp. 152–55.

3 Jean Laplanche, 'To Situate Sublimation', trans. Richard Miller, *October*, no. 28, Spring 1984, pp. 7–26.

4 Freud briefly returns to sublimation in his paper 'Moses and Monotheism: Three Essays', 1939, in which he characterises Moses as an example of sublimation of the highest order, again because of a capacity to adhere to an abstraction, i.e. an abstract God.

5 Darian Leader, *Stealing the Mona Lisa: What Art Stops Us from Seeing*, Faber and Faber, 2002, p. 113.

6 See Leo Barsani, *The Freudian Body: Psychoanalysis and Art*, Columbia University Press, 1986.

PREFACE TO THE 1922 EDITION

With a book already so well-known little seems needed by way of Preface. It is a brilliant example of the way in which knowledge based on the detailed psycho-analysis of living persons can be made use of to throw light on the deeper springs of character in those whose mind is not accessible to direct investigation. The process is, therefore, akin to a piece of archaeological reconstruction. The study is based on the solitary mention Leonardo makes of his childhood, evidence which most psychologists would have passed by as being flimsy and meaningless; but its unique occurrence and extraordinary nature both call for explanation, if we are not to dismiss such happenings as being causeless. Professor Freud has dealt with it by comparing it with similar phantasies analysed by him and with other known facts of Leonardo's life. In the fascinating study resulting from this procedure he has thrown a flood of light on one of the most remarkable and interesting personalities of history.

Ernest Jones.
December, 1921.

EDITOR'S NOTE

EINE KINDHEITSERINNERUNG DES LEONARDO DA VINCI

   (a) German Editions:

1910 Leipzig and Vienna: Deuticke. Pp. 71. (*Schriften zur angewandten Seelenkunde*, Heft 7)

1919 2nd ed. Same publishers. Pp. 76.

1923 3rd ed. Same publishers. Pp. 78.

1925 G.S., **9**, 371–454.

1943 G.W., **8**, 128–211.

   (b) English Translation:

Leonardo da Vinci

1916 New York: Moffat, Yard. Pp. 130. (Tr. A. A. Brill.)

1922 London: Kegan Paul. Pp. v + 130. (Same translator, with a preface by Ernest Jones.)

1932 New York: Dodd Mead. Pp. 138. (Re-issue of above.)

The present translation, with a modified title, 'Leonardo da Vinci and a Memory of his Childhood', is an entirely new one by Alan Tyson.

That Freud's interest in Leonardo was of long standing is shown by a sentence in a letter to Fliess of October 9, 1898 (Freud, 1950a, Letter 98), in which he remarked that 'perhaps the most famous left-handed individual was Leonardo, who is not known to have had any love-affairs'.[1] This interest, furthermore, was not a passing one, for we find in Freud's reply to a 'questionnaire' on his favourite books (1907d) that he mentions among them Merezhkovsky's study of Leonardo. But the immediate stimulus to writing the present work appears to have come in the autumn of 1909 from one of his patients who, as he remarked in a letter to Jung on October 17, seemed to have the same constitution as Leonardo without his genius. He added that he was obtaining a book on Leonardo's youth from Italy. This was the monograph by Scognamiglio referred to on p. 29n. After reading this and some other books on Leonardo, he spoke on the subject to the Vienna Psycho-Analytical Society on December 1; but it was not until the beginning of April, 1910, that he finished writing his study. It was published at the end of May.

Freud made a number of corrections and additions in the later issues of the book. Among these may be specially mentioned the short footnote on circumcision (p. 46n), the excerpt from Reitler (pp. 16–17n), and the long quotation from Pfister (pp. 70–2n), all of them added in 1919, and the discussion of the London cartoon (pp. 69–70n), added in 1923.

This work of Freud's was not the first application of the methods of clinical psycho-analysis to the lives of historical figures in the

---

[1] A connection between bilaterality and bisexuality had been asserted by Fliess but questioned by Freud. An indirect reference to this controversy (which was one of the occasions for their estrangement) will be found on p. 95 below.

past. Experiments in this direction had already been made by others, notably by Sadger, who had published studies on Conrad Ferdinand Meyer (1908), Lenau (1909) and Kleist (1909).[1] Freud himself had never before embarked on a full-length biographical study of this kind, though he had previously made a few fragmentary analyses of writers, based on episodes in their works. Long before this, in fact on June 20, 1898, he had sent Fliess a study of one of C. F. Meyer's short stories, 'Die Richterin', which threw light on its author's early life (Freud, 1950a, Letter 91). But this monograph on Leonardo was not only in the field of biography. The book seems to have been greeted with more than the usual amount of disapproval, and Freud was evidently justified in defending himself in advance with the reflections at the beginning of Chapter VI (p. 88)—reflections which have a general application even to-day to the authors and critics of biographies.

It is a strange fact, however, that until very recently none of the critics of the present work seem to have lighted upon what is no doubt its weakest point. A prominent part is played by Leonardo's memory or phantasy of being visited in his cradle by a bird of prey. The name applied to this bird in his notebooks is 'nibio', which (in the modern form of 'nibbio') is the ordinary Italian word for 'kite'. Freud, however, throughout his study translates the word by the German 'Geier', for which the English can only be 'vulture'.[2]

Freud's mistake seems to have originated from some of the German translations which he used. Thus Marie Herzfeld

---

[1] The minutes of the Vienna Psycho-Analytical Society (which we are unfortunately precluded from quoting) show that at a meeting on December 11, 1907, Freud made some remarks on the subject of psycho-analytic biography. (Cf. Jones, 1955, 383.)

[2] This was pointed out by Irma Richter in a footnote to her recently published selection from Leonardo's Notebooks (1952, 286) Like Pfister (p. 72n. below), she refers to Leonardo's childhood memory as a 'dream'.

(1906) uses the word '*Geier*' in one of her versions of the cradle phantasy instead of '*Milan*', the normal German word for 'kite'. But probably the most important influence was the German translation of Merezhkovsky's Leonardo book which, as may be seen from the marked copy in Freud's library, was the source of a very great deal of his information about Leonardo and in which he probably came across the story for the first time. Here too the German word used in the cradle phantasy is '*Geier*', though Merezhkovsky himself correctly used '*korshun*', the Russian word for 'kite'.

In face of this mistake, some readers may feel an impulse to dismiss the whole study as worthless. It will, however, be a good plan to examine the situation more coolly and consider in detail the exact respects in which Freud's arguments and conclusions are invalidated.

In the first place the 'hidden bird' in Leonardo's picture (p. 70n.) must be abandoned. If it is a bird at all, it is a vulture; it bears no resemblance to a kite. This 'discovery', however, was not made by Freud but by Pfister. It was not introduced until the second edition of the work, and Freud received it with considerable reserve.

Next, and more important, comes the Egyptian connection. The hieroglyph for the Egyptian word for 'mother' ('*mut*') quite certainly represents a vulture and not a kite. Gardiner in his authoritative *Egyptian Grammar* (2nd ed., 1950, 469) identifies the creature as '*Gyps fulvus*', the griffon vulture. It follows from this that Freud's theory that the bird of Leonardo's phantasy stood for his mother cannot claim direct support from the Egyptian myth, and that the question of his acquaintance with that myth ceases to be relevant.[1] The phantasy and the myth seem to have

[1] Nor can the story of the virginal impregnation of vultures serve as evidence of Leonardo's having had an exclusive bond with his mother in his infancy—though the existence of that bond is not contradicted by the failure of this particular evidence.

no immediate connection with each other. Nevertheless each of them, taken independently, raises an interesting problem. How was it that the ancient Egyptians came to link up the ideas of 'vulture' and 'mother'? Does the egyptologists' explanation that it is merely a matter of a chance phonetic coincidence meet the question? If not, Freud's discussion of androgynous mother-goddesses must have a value of its own, irrespective of its connection with the case of Leonardo. So too Leonardo's phantasy of the bird visiting him in his cradle and putting its tail into his mouth continues to cry out for an explanation even if the bird was not a vulture. And Freud's psychological analysis of the phantasy is not contradicted by this correction but merely deprived of one piece of corroborative support.

Apart, then, from the consequent irrelevance of the Egyptian discussion—though this nevertheless retains much of its independent value—the main body of Freud's study is unaffected by his mistake: the detailed construction of Leonardo's emotional life from his earliest years, the account of the conflict between his artistic and his scientific impulses, the deep analysis of his psychosexual history. And, in addition to this main topic, the study presents us with a number of not less important side-themes: a more general discussion of the nature and workings of the mind of the creative artist, an outline of the genesis of one particular type of homosexuality, and—of special interest to the history of psycho-analytic theory—the first full emergence of the concept of narcissism.

1

When psychiatric research, normally content to draw on frailer men for its material, approaches one who is among the greatest of the human race, it is not doing so for the reasons so frequently ascribed to it by laymen. 'To blacken the radiant and drag the sublime into the dust' is no part of its purpose,[1] and there is no satisfaction for it in narrowing the gulf which separates the perfection of the great from the inadequacy of the objects that are its usual concern. But it cannot help finding worthy of understanding everything that can be recognized in those illustrious models, and it believes there is no one so great as to be disgraced by being subject to the laws which govern both normal and pathological activity with equal cogency.

[1] [Es liebt die Welt, das Strahlende zu schwärzen
    Und das Erhabene in den Staub zu ziehn.
    (The world loves to blacken the radiant and drag the sublime into the dust.)

From a poem by Schiller, 'Das Mädchen von Orleans', inserted as an extra prologue to the 1801 edition of his play Die Jungfrau von Orleans. The poem is reputed to have been an attack on Voltaire's La Pucelle.]

Leonardo da Vinci (1452–1519) was admired even by his contemporaries as one of the greatest men of the Italian renaissance; yet in their time he had already begun to seem an enigma, just as he does to us to-day. He was a universal genius 'whose outlines can only be surmised,—never defined'.[1] In his own time his most decisive influence was in painting, and it was left to us to recognize the greatness of the natural scientist (and engineer)[2] that was combined in him with the artist. Though he left behind him masterpieces of painting, while his scientific discoveries remained unpublished and unused, the investigator in him never in the course of his development left the artist entirely free, but often made severe encroachments on him and perhaps in the end suppressed him. In the last hour of his life, according to the words that Vasari gives him, he reproached himself with having offended God and man by his failure to do his duty in his art.[3] And even if this story of Vasari's has neither external nor much internal probability but belongs to the legend which began to be woven around the mysterious Master even before his death, it is still of incontestable value as evidence of what men believed at the time.

What was it that prevented Leonardo's personality from being understood by his contemporaries? The cause of this was certainly not the versatility of his talents and the range of his knowledge, which enabled him to introduce himself to the court of the Duke of Milan, Lodovico Sforza, called Il Moro, as

[1] The words are Jacob Burckhardt's, quoted by Konstantinowa (1907, [51]).

[2] [The words in parentheses were added in 1923.]

[3] 'Egli per reverenza, rizzatosi a sedere sul letto, contando il mal suo e gli accidenti di quello, mostrava tuttavia quanto avea offeso Dio e gli uomini del mondo, non avendo operato nell' arte come si conveniva.' ['He having raised himself out of reverence so as to sit on the bed, and giving an account of his illness and its circumstances, yet showed how much he had offended God and mankind in not having worked at his art as he should have done.'] Vasari [ed. Poggi, 1919, 43].

a performer on a kind of lute of his own invention, or allowed him to write the remarkable letter to the same duke in which he boasted of his achievements as architect and military engineer. For the days of the renaissance were quite familiar with such a combination of wide and diverse abilities in a single individual—though we must allow that Leonardo himself was one of the most brilliant examples of this. Nor did he belong to the type of genius who has received a niggardly outward endowment from Nature, and who in his turn places no value on the outward forms of life, but in a spirit of painful gloom flies from all dealings with mankind. On the contrary, he was tall and well-proportioned; his features were of consummate beauty and his physical strength unusual; he was charming in his manner, supremely eloquent, and cheerful and amiable to everyone. He loved beauty in the things that surrounded him; he was fond of magnificent clothing and valued every refinement of living. In a passage from the treatise on painting, which reveals his lively capacity for enjoyment, he compares painting with its sister arts and describes the hardships that await the sculptor: 'For his face is smeared and dusted all over with marble powder so that he looks like a baker, and he is completely covered with little chips of marble, so that it seems as if his back had been snowed on; and his house is full of splinters of stone and dust. In the case of the painter it is quite different . . . for the painter sits in front of his work in perfect comfort. He is well-dressed and handles the lightest of brushes which he dips in pleasant colours. He wears the clothes he likes; and his house is full of delightful paintings, and is spotlessly clean. He is often accompanied by music or by men who read from a variety of beautiful works, and he can listen to these with great pleasure and without the din of hammers and other noises.'[1]

[1] *Trattato della Pittura* [Ludwig (1909, 36); also Richter, I. A. (1952, 330f.)].

It is indeed quite possible that the idea of a radiantly happy and pleasure-loving Leonardo is only applicable to the first and longer period of the artist's life. Afterwards, when the downfall of Lodovico Moro's rule forced him to leave Milan, the city that was the centre of his activity and where his position was assured, and to pursue a life lacking in security and not rich in external successes, until he found his last asylum in France, the sparkle of his temperament may have grown dim and some strange sides of his nature may have been thrown into prominence. Moreover the turning of his interests from his art to science, which increased as time went on, must have played its part in widening the gulf between himself and his contemporaries. All the efforts in which in their opinion he frittered away his time when he could have been industriously painting to order and becoming rich (as, for example, his former fellow-student Perugina did) seemed to them to be merely capricious trifling or even caused him to be suspected of being in the service of the 'black art'. We are in a position to understand him better, for we know from his notes what were the arts he practised. In an age which was beginning to replace the authority of the Church by that of antiquity and which was not yet familiar with any form of research not based on presuppositions, Leonardo—the forerunner and by no means unworthy rival of Bacon and Copernicus—was necessarily isolated. In his dissection of the dead bodies of horses and human beings, in his construction of flying machines, and in his studies on the nutrition of plants and their reactions to poisons, he certainly departed widely from the commentators on Aristotle, and came close to the despised alchemists, in whose laboratories experimental research had found some refuge at least in those unfavourable times.

The effect that this had on his painting was that he took up his brush with reluctance, painted less and less, left what he had begun for the most part unfinished and cared little about the ultimate fate of his works. And this was what he was blamed for by his contemporaries: to them his attitude towards his art remained a riddle.

Several of Leonardo's later admirers have made attempts to acquit his character of the flaw of instability. In his defence they claim that he is blamed for what is a general feature of great artists: even the energetic Michelangelo, a man entirely given up to his labours, left many of his works incomplete, and it was no more his fault than it was Leonardo's in the parallel instance. Moreover, in the case of some of the pictures, they urge, it is not so much a question of their being unfinished as of his declaring them to be so. What appears to the layman as a masterpiece is never for the creator of the work of art more than an unsatisfactory embodiment of what he intended; he has some dim notion of a perfection, whose likeness time and again he despairs of reproducing. Least of all, they claim, is it right to make the artist responsible for the ultimate fate of his works.

Valid as some of these excuses may be, they still do not cover the whole state of affairs that confronts us in Leonardo. The same distressing struggle with a work, the final flight from it and the indifference to its future fate may recur in many other artists, but there is no doubt that this behaviour is shown in Leonardo in an extreme degree. Solmi (1910, 12) quotes the remark of one of his pupils: 'Pareva che ad ogni ora tremasse, quando si poneva a dipingere, e però non diede mai fine ad alcuna cosa cominciata, considerando la grandezza dell'arte, tal che egli scorgeva errori in quelle cose, che ad altri parevano miracoli.'[1] His last pictures, he goes on, the Leda, the Madonna di Sant' Onofrio, Bacchus, and the young St. John the Baptist, remained unfinished 'come

[1] ['He appeared to tremble the whole time when he set himself to paint, and yet he never completed any work he had begun, having so high a regard for the greatness of art that he discovered faults in things that to others seemed miracles.']

quasi intervenne di tutte le cose sue . . . '[1] Lomazzo, who made
a copy of the Last Supper, refers in a sonnet to Leonardo's
notorious inability to finish his works:

> Protogen che il pennel di sue pitture
> Non levava, agguaglio il Vinci Divo
> Di cui opra non è finita pure.[2]

The slowness with which Leonardo worked was proverbial.
He painted at the Last Supper in the Convent of Santa Maria delle
Grazie in Milan, after the most thorough preparatory studies, for
three whole years. One of his contemporaries, Matteo Bandelli,
the story-writer, who at the time was a young monk in the
convent, tells how Leonardo often used to climb up the scaffold-
ing early in the morning and remain there till twilight never
once laying his brush aside, and with no thought of eating or
drinking. Then days would pass without his putting his hand to
it. Sometimes he would remain for hours in front of the painting, merely examining it in his mind. At other times he would
come straight to the convent from the court in the castle at
Milan, where he was making the model of the equestrian statue
for Francesco Sforza, in order to add a few strokes of the brush to
a figure, and then immediately break off.[3] According to Vasari he
spent four years in painting the portrait of Mona Lisa, the wife of
the Florentine Francesco del Giocondo, without being able to
bring it to final completion. This circumstance may also account
for the fact that the picture was never delivered to the man who
commissioned it, but instead remained with Leonardo and was

---

[1] ['As happened more or less to all his works.']

[2] ['Protogenes, who never lifted his brush from his work, was the equal of the
divine Vinci, who never finished anything at all.'] Quoted by Scognamiglio
(1900, [112]).

[3] Von Seidlitz (1909, **1**,203).

taken to France by him.[1] It was bought by King Francis I, and to-day forms one of the greatest treasures of the Louvre.

If these reports of the way in which Leonardo worked are compared with the evidence of the extraordinarily numerous sketches and studies which he left behind him and which exhibit every *motif* appearing in his paintings in a great variety of forms, we are bound totally to reject the idea that traits of hastiness and unsteadiness acquired the slightest influence over Leonardo's relation to his art. On the contrary, it is possible to observe a quite extraordinary profundity, a wealth of possibilities between which a decision can only be reached with hesitation, demands which can hardly be satisfied, and an inhibition in the actual execution which is not in fact to be explained even by the artist inevitably falling short of his ideal. The slowness which had all along been conspicuous in Leonardo's work is seen to be a symptom of this inhibition and to be the forerunner of his subsequent withdrawal from painting.[2] It was this too which determined the fate of the Last Supper—a fate that was not undeserved. Leonardo could not become reconciled to fresco painting, which demands rapid work while the ground is still moist, and this was the reason why he chose oil colours, the drying of which permitted him to protract the completion of the painting to suit his mood and leisure. These pigments however detached themselves from the ground on which they were applied and which separated them from the wall. Added to this, the defects in the wall, and the later fortunes of the building itself, determined what seems to be the inevitable ruin of the picture.[3]

The miscarriage of a similar technical experiment appears to

[1] Von Seidlitz (1909, **2**, 48).

[2] Pater [1873, 100]: 'But it is certain that at one period of his life he had almost ceased to be an artist.'

[3] See von Seidlitz (1909, **1**, [205 ff.]) for the history of the attempts to restore and preserve the picture.

have caused the destruction of the Battle of Anghiari, the painting which, in competition with Michelangelo, he began to paint some time afterwards on a wall of the Sala del Consiglio in Florence, and which he also abandoned in an unfinished condition. Here it seems as if an alien interest—in experimentation—at first reinforced the artistic one, only to damage the work later on.

The character of Leonardo the man showed some other unusual traits and apparent contradictions. A certain inactivity and indifference seemed obvious in him. At a time when everyone was trying to gain the widest scope for his activity—a goal unattainable without the development of energetic aggressiveness towards other people—Leonardo was notable for his quiet peaceableness and his avoidance of all antagonism and controversy. He was gentle and kindly to everyone; he declined, it is said, to eat meat, since he did not think it justifiable to deprive animals of their lives; and he took particular pleasure in buying birds in the market and setting them free.[1] He condemned war and bloodshed and described man as not so much the king of the animal world but rather the worst of the wild beasts.[2] But this feminine delicacy of feeling did not deter him from accompanying condemned criminals on their way to execution in order to study their features distorted by fear and to sketch them in his notebook. Nor did it stop him from devising the cruellest offensive weapons and from entering the service of Cesare Borgia as chief military engineer. He often gave the appearance of being indifferent to good and evil, or he insisted on measurement by a special standard. He accompanied Cesare in a position of authority during the campaign that brought the Romagna into the

[1] Müntz (1899, 18). A letter of a contemporary from India to one of the Medici alludes to this characteristic behaviour of Leonardo. (See J. P. Richter [1939, 2, 103–4n.)
[2] Bottazzi (1910, 186).

possession of that most ruthless and faithless of adversaries. There is not a line in Leonardo's notebooks which reveals any criticism of the events of those days, or any concern in them. A comparison suggests itself here with Goethe during the French campaign.

If a biographical study is really intended to arrive at an understanding of its hero's mental life it must not—as happens in the majority of biographies as a result of discretion or prudishness—silently pass over its subject's sexual activity or sexual individuality. What is known of Leonardo in this respect is little: but that little is full of significance. In an age which saw a struggle between sensuality without restraint and gloomy asceticism, Leonardo represented the cool repudiation of sexuality—a thing that would scarcely be expected of an artist and a portrayer of feminine beauty. Solmi quotes the following sentence of his which is evidence of his frigidity: 'The act of procreation and everything connected with it is so disgusting that mankind would soon die out if it were not an old-established custom and if there were not pretty faces and sensuous natures.'[1] His posthumous writings, which not only deal with the greatest scientific problems but also contain trivialities that strike us as scarcely worthy of so great a mind (an allegorical natural history, animal fables, jokes, prophecies),[2] are chaste—one might say even abstinent—to a degree that would cause surprise in a work of *belles lettres* even to-day. So resolutely do they shun everything sexual that it would seem as if Eros alone, the preserver of all living things, was not worthy material for the investigator in his pursuit of knowledge.[3] It is well known how frequently

[1] Solmi (1908, [24]).

[2] Herzfeld (1906).

[3] An exception to this (though an unimportant one) is perhaps to be found in his collected witticisms—*belle facezie*—which have not been translated. See Herzfeld (1906, 151).—[This reference to Eros as 'the preserver of all living things' seems to anticipate Freud's introduction of the name ten years later, in

great artists take pleasure in giving vent to their phantasies in erotic and even crudely obscene pictures. In Leonardo's case on the contrary we have some anatomical sketches of the internal female genitals, the position of the embryo in the womb and so on.[1]

almost exactly the same phrase, as a general term for the sexual as opposed to the death instincts. See, for instance, *Beyond the Pleasure Principle* (1920g) *Standard Ed.*, **18**, 50 and 52.]

[1] [*Footnote added* 1919:] Some remarkable errors are visible in a drawing made by Leonardo of the sexual act seen in anatomical sagittal section, which certainly cannot be called obscene [Fig. 1]. They were discovered by Reitler (1917) and discussed by him in the light of the account which I have given here of Leonardo's character:

'It is precisely in the process of portraying the act of procreation that this excessive instinct for research has totally failed—obviously only as a result of his even greater sexual repression. The man's body is drawn in full, the woman's only in part. If the drawing reproduced in Fig. 1 is shown to an unprejudiced onlooker with the head visible but all the lower parts covered up, it may be safely assumed that the head will be taken to be a woman's. The wavy locks on the forehead, and the others, which flow down the back approximately to the fourth or fifth dorsal vertebra, mark the head as more of a woman's than a man's.

'The woman's breast reveals two defects. The first indeed is an artistic one, for its outline gives it the appearance of a breast that is flabby and hangs down unpleasingly. The second defect is anatomical, for Leonardo the researcher had obviously been prevented by his fending off of sexuality from ever making a close examination of a nursing woman's nipples. Had he done so he would have been bound to notice that the milk flows out a number of separate excretory ducts. Leonardo, however, drew only a single duct extending far down into the abdominal cavity and probably in his view drawing the milk from the *cisterna chyli* and perhaps also connected in some way with the sex organs. It must of course be taken into consideration that the study of the internal organs of the human body was at that time made extremely difficult, since the dissection of bodies was regarded as desecration of the dead and was most severely punished. Whether Leonardo, who had certainly only very little material for dissection at his disposal, knew anything at all of the existence of a lymph-reservoir in the abdominal cavity is therefore in fact highly questionable, although in his drawing he included a cavity that is no doubt intended to

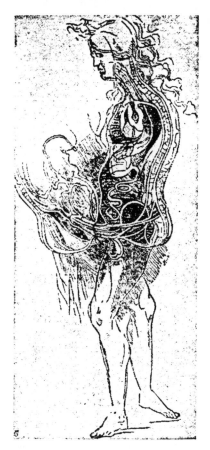

Figure 1

It is doubtful whether Leonardo ever embraced a woman in passion; nor is it known that he had any intimate mental relationship with a woman, such as Michelangelo's with Vittoria

be something of the sort. But from his making the lactiferous duct extend still further downwards till it reaches the internal sex organs we may suspect that he was trying to represent the synchronization of the beginning of the secretion

Colonna. While he was still an apprentice, living in the house of
his master Verrocchio, a charge of forbidden homosexual prac-
tices was brought against him, along with some other young

of milk and the end of pregnancy by means of visible anatomical connections
as well. However, even if we are ready to excuse the artist's defective knowledge
of anatomy by referring it to the circumstances of his time, the striking fact still
remains that it is precisely the female genital that Leonardo has treated so
carelessly. The vagina and something that looks like the *portio uteri* can no doubt
be made out, but the lines indicating the uterus itself are completely confused.

'The male genital on the other hand is depicted by Leonardo much more
correctly. Thus, for instance, he was not satisfied with drawing the testis but
also put in the epididymis, which he drew with perfect accuracy.

'What is especially remarkable is the posture in which Leonardo makes
coitus take place. Picture and drawings by famous artists exist which depict
coitus a tergo, a latere, etc., but when it comes to a drawing of the sexual act being
performed standing up, we must surely suppose that there was a sexual repression of quite special strength to have caused it to be represented in this isolated
and almost grotesque way. If one wants to enjoy oneself it is usual to make
oneself as comfortable as possible: this of course is true for both the primal
instincts, hunger and love. Most of the peoples of antiquity took their meals in
a lying position and it is normal in coitus to-day to lie down just as comfortably
as did our ancestors. Lying down implies more or less a wish to stay in the
desired situation for some time.

'Moreover the features of the man with the feminine head are marked by a
resistance that is positively indignant. His brows are wrinkled and his gaze is
directed sideways with an expression of repugnance. The lips are pressed
together and their corners are then drawn down. In this face can be seen
neither the pleasure of love's blessings nor the happiness of indulgence: it
expresses only indignation and aversion.

'The clumsiest blunder, however, was made by Leonardo in drawing the two
lower extremities. The man's foot should in point of fact have been his right
one; for since Leonardo depicted the act of union in an anatomical sagittal
section it follows of course that the man's left foot would be above the plane of
the picture. Conversely, and for the same reason, the woman's foot should have
belonged to her left side. But in fact Leonardo has interchanged male and
female. The male figure has a left foot and the female one a right foot. This
interchange is easiest to grasp if one recalls that the big toes lie on the inner
sides of the feet.

people, which ended in his acquittal. He seems to have fallen under this suspicion because he had employed a boy of bad reputation as a model.[1] When he had become a Master, he surrounded himself with handsome boys and youths whom he took as pupils. The last of these pupils, Francesco Melzi, accompanied him to France, remained with him up to his death and was named by him as his heir. Without sharing in the certainty of his modern biographers, who naturally reject the possibility that there was a sexual relationship between him and his pupils as a baseless insult to the great man, we may take it as much more probable that Leonardo's affectionate relations with the young men who—as was the custom with pupils at that time—shared his existence did not extend to sexual activity. Moreover a high degree of sexual activity is not to be attributed to him.

There is only one way in which the peculiarity of this emotional and sexual life can be understood in connection with Leonardo's double nature as an artist and as a scientific investigator. Among his biographers, to whom a psychological approach is often very alien, there is to my knowledge only one, Edmondo Solmi, who has approached the solution of the problem; but a writer who has chosen Leonardo as the hero of a great historical novel, Dmitry Sergeyevich Merezhkovsky, has made a similar

---

'This anatomical drawing alone would have made it possible to deduce the repression of libido—a repression which threw the great artist and investigator into something approaching confusion.'

[*Added* 1923:] These remarks of Reitler's have been criticized, it is true, on the ground that such serious conclusions should not be drawn from a hasty sketch, and that it is not even certain whether the different parts of the drawing really belong together.

[1] According to Scognamiglio (1900, 49) there is a reference to this episode in an obscure and even variously read passage in the Codex Atlanticus: 'Quando io feci Domeneddio putto voi mi metteste in prigione, ora s'io lo fo grande, voi mi farete peggio.' ['When I represented the Lord God as a baby, you put me in prison; now if I represent him as an adult you will do worse to me.']

reading of this unusual man the basis of his portrait and has given clear expression to his conception, not indeed in plain language, but (after the way of writers of imagination) in plastic terms.[1] Solmi's verdict on Leonardo is as follows (1908, 46): 'But his insatiable desire to understand everything around him, and to fathom in a spirit of cold superiority the deepest secret of all that is perfect, had condemned Leonardo's work to remain for ever unfinished.'

In an essay in the *Conferenze Fiorentine* the following pronouncement of Leonardo's is quoted, which represents his confession of faith and provides the key to his nature: 'Nessuna cosa si può amare nè odiare, se prima non si ha cognition di quella.'[2] That is to say: One has no right to love or hate anything if one has not acquired a thorough knowledge of its nature. And the same is repeated by Leonardo in a passage in the treatise on painting where he seems to be defending himself against the charge of irreligion: 'But such carping critics would do better to keep silent. For that (line of conduct) is the way to become acquainted with the Creator of so many wonderful things, and this is the way to love so great an Inventor. For in truth great love springs from great knowledge of the beloved object, and if you know it but little you will be able to love it only a little or not at all . . . '[3]

The value of these remarks of Leonardo's is not to be looked for in their conveying an important psychological fact; for what they assert is obviously false, and Leonardo must have known this as well as we do. It is not true that human beings delay loving or hating until they have studied and become familiar with the nature of the object to which these affects apply. On the

[1] Merezhkovsky (1902; German trans., 1903). *Leonardo da Vinci* forms the second work of a great historical trilogy entitled *Christ and Antichrist*. The two other volumes are *Julian the Apostate* and *Peter and Alexis*.

[2] Bottazzi (1910, 193) [J. P. Richter (1939, 2, 244)].

[3] *Trattato della Pittura* [Ludwig (1909, 54)].

contrary they love impulsively, from emotional motives which have nothing to do with knowledge, and whose operation is at most weakened by reflection and consideration. Leonardo, then, could only have meant that the love practised by human beings was not of the proper and unobjectionable kind: one *should* love in such a way as to hold back the affect, subject it to the process of reflection and only let it take its course when it has stood up to the test of thought. And at the same time we understand that he wishes to tell us that it happens so in his case and that it would be worth while for everyone else to treat love and hatred as he does.

And in his case it really seems to have been so. His affects were controlled and subjected to the instinct for research; he did not love and hate, but asked himself about the origin and significance of what he was to love or hate. Thus he was bound at first to appear indifferent to good and evil, beauty and ugliness. During this work of investigation love and hate threw off their positive or negative signs and were both alike transformed into intellectual interest. In reality Leonardo was not devoid of passion; he did not lack the divine spark which is directly or indirectly the driving force—*il primo motore*—behind all human activity. He had merely converted his passion into a thirst for knowledge; he then applied himself to investigation with the persistence, constancy and penetration which is derived from passion, and at the climax of intellectual labour, when knowledge had been won, he allowed the long restrained affect to break loose and to flow away freely, as a stream of water drawn from a river is allowed to flow away when its work is done. When, at the climax of a discovery, he could survey a large portion of the whole nexus, he was overcome by emotion, and in ecstatic language praised the splendour of the part of creation that he had studied, or—in religious phraseology—the greatness of his Creator. This process of transformation in Leonardo has been rightly understood by Solmi. After quoting a passage of this sort in which Leonardo celebrates the sublime law of nature ('O mirabile necessità . . .'), he writes (1910, 11): 'Tale trasfigurazione della scienza della natura in emozione, quasi direi, religiosa, è uno dei tratti caratteristici de' manoscritti vinciani, e si trova cento e cento volte espressa . . .'[1]

Because of his insatiable and indefatigable thirst for knowledge Leonardo has been called the Italian Faust. But quite apart from doubts about a possible transformation of the instinct to investigate back into an enjoyment of life—a transformation which we must take as fundamental in the tragedy of Faust—the view may be hazarded that Leonardo's development approaches Spinoza's mode of thinking.

A conversion of psychical instinctual force into various forms of activity can perhaps no more be achieved without loss than a conversion of physical forces. The example of Leonardo teaches us how many other things we have to take into account in connection with these processes. The postponement of loving until full knowledge is acquired ends in a substitution of the latter for the former. A man who has won his way to a state of knowledge cannot properly be said to love and hate; he remains beyond love and hatred. He has investigated instead of loving. And that is perhaps why Leonardo's life was so much poorer in love than that of other great men, and of other artists. The stormy passions of a nature that inspires and consumes, passions in which other men have enjoyed their richest experience, appear not to have touched him.

There are some further consequences. Investigating has taken the place of acting and creating as well. A man who has begun to have an inkling of the grandeur of the universe with all its complexities and its laws readily forgets his own insignificant self.

---

[1] ['Such a transfiguration of natural science into a sort of religious emotion is one of the characteristic features of Leonardo's manuscripts, and there are hundreds and hundreds of examples of it.']

Lost in admiration and filled with true humility, he all too easily forgets that he himself is a part of those active forces and that in accordance with the scale of his personal strength the way is open for him to try to alter a small portion of the destined course of the world—a world in which the small is still no less wonderful and significant than the great.

Leonardo's researches had perhaps first begun, as Solmi believes, in the service of his art;[1] he directed his efforts to the properties and laws of light, colours, shadows and perspective in order to ensure mastery in the imitation of nature and to point the same way to others. It is probable that at that time he already overrated the value to the artist of these branches of knowledge. Still constantly following the lead given by the requirements of his painting he was then driven to investigate the painter's subjects, animals and plants, and the proportions of the human body, and, passing from their exterior, to proceed to gain a knowledge of their internal structure and their vital functions, which indeed also find expression in their appearance and have a claim to be depicted in art. And finally the instinct, which had become overwhelming, swept him away until the connection with the demands of his art was severed, so that he discovered the general laws of mechanics and divined the history of the stratification and fossilization in the Arno valley, and until he could enter in large letters in his book the discovery: *Il sole non si move.*[2] His investigations extended to practically every branch of natural science, and in every single one he was a discoverer or at

---

[1] Solmi (1910, 8): 'Leonardo aveva posto, come regola al pittore, lo studio della natura . . . poi la passione dello studio era divenuta dominante, egli aveva voluto acquistare non più la scienza per l'arte, ma la scienza per la scienza.' ['Leonardo had prescribed the study of nature as a rule for the painter . . ., then the passion for study had become dominant, he had no longer wished to acquire learning for the sake of art, but learning for the sake of learning.']

[2] ['The sun does not move.' Quaderni d'Anatomia, 1–6, Royal Library, Windsor, V, 25.]

least a prophet and pioneer.[1] Yet his urge for knowledge was always directed to the external world; something kept him far away from the investigation of the human mind. In the 'Academia Vinciana' [p. 87], for which he drew some cleverly intertwined emblems, there was little room for psychology.

Then, when he made the attempt to return from investigation to his starting point, the exercise of his art, he found himself disturbed by the new direction of his interests and the changed nature of his mental activity. What interested him in a picture was above all a problem; and behind the first one he saw countless other problems arising, just as he used to in his endless and inexhaustible investigation of nature. He was no longer able to limit his demands, to see the work of art in isolation and to tear it from the wide context to which he knew it belonged. After the most exhausting efforts to bring to expression in it everything which was connected with it in his thoughts, he was forced to abandon it in an unfinished state or to declare that it was incomplete.

The artist had once taken the investigator into his service to assist him; now the servant had become the stronger and suppressed his master.

When we find that in the picture presented by a person's character a single instinct has developed an excessive strength, as did the craving for knowledge in Leonardo, we look for the explanation in a special disposition—though about its determinants (which are probably organic) scarcely anything is yet known. Our psycho-analytic studies of neurotic people have however led us to form two further expectations which it would be gratifying to find confirmed in each particular case. We consider it probable that an instinct like this of excessive strength

---

[1] See the enumeration of his scientific achievements in the fine biographical introduction by Marie Herzfeld (1906), in the various essays of the *Conferenze Fiorentine* (1910), and elsewhere.

was already active in the subject's earliest childhood, and that
its supremacy was established by impressions in the child's life.
We make the further assumption that it found reinforcement
from what were originally sexual instinctual forces, so that later
it could take the place of a part of the subject's sexual life. Thus
a person of this sort would, for example, pursue research with
the same passionate devotion that another would give to his
love, and he would be able to investigate instead of loving. We
would venture to infer that it is not only in the example of the
instinct to investigate that there has been a sexual reinforcement, but also in most other cases where an instinct is of
special intensity.

Observation of men's daily lives shows us that most people
succeed in directing very considerable portions of their sexual
instinctual forces to their professional activity. The sexual
instinct is particularly well fitted to make contributions of this
kind since it is endowed with a capacity for sublimation: that is,
it has the power to replace its immediate aim by other aims
which may be valued more highly and which are not sexual. We
accept this process as proved whenever the history of a person's
childhood—that is, the history of his mental development—
shows that in childhood this over-powerful instinct was in the
service of sexual interests. We find further confirmation if a
striking atrophy occurs in the sexual life of maturity, as though a
portion of sexual activity had now been replaced by the activity
of the over-powerful instinct.

There seem to be special difficulties in applying these expectations to the case of an over-powerful instinct for investigation,
since precisely in the case of children there is a reluctance to
credit them with either this serious instinct or any noteworthy
sexual interests. However, these difficulties are easily overcome.
The curiosity of small children is manifested in their untiring
love of asking questions; this is bewildering to the adult so long
as he fails to understand that all these questions are merely

circumlocutions and that they cannot come to an end because the child is only trying to make them take the place of a question which he does not ask. When he grows bigger and becomes better informed this expression of curiosity often comes to a sudden end. Psycho-analytic investigation provides us with a full explanation by teaching us that many, perhaps most children, or at least most gifted ones, pass through a period, beginning when they are about three, which may be called the period of *infantile sexual researches*. So far as we know, the curiosity of children of this age does not awaken spontaneously, but is aroused by the impression made by some important event—by the actual birth of a little brother or sister, or by fear of it based on external experiences—in which the child perceives a threat to his selfish interests. Researches are directed to the question of where babies come from, exactly as if the child were looking for ways and means to avert so undesired an event. In this way we have been astonished to learn that children refuse to believe the bits of information that are given them—for example that they energetically reject the fable of the stork with its wealth of mythological meaning—, that they date their intellectual independence from this act of disbelief, and that they often feel in serious opposition to adults and in fact never afterwards forgive them for having deceived them here about the true facts of the case. They investigate along their own lines, divine the baby's presence inside its mother's body, and following the lead of the impulses of their own sexuality form theories of babies originating from eating, of their being born through the bowels, and of the obscure part played by the father. By that time they already have a notion of the sexual act, which appears to them to be something hostile and violent. But since their own sexual constitution has not yet reached the point of being able to produce babies, their investigation of where babies come from must inevitably come to nothing too and be abandoned as insoluble. The impression caused by this failure in the first attempt at intellectual independence appears to be of a lasting and deeply depressing kind.[1]

When the period of infantile sexual researches has been terminated by a wave of energetic sexual repression, the instinct for research has three distinct possible vicissitudes open to it owing to its early connection with sexual interests. In the first of these, research shares the fate of sexuality; thenceforward curiosity remains inhibited and the free activity of intelligence may be limited for the whole of the subject's lifetime, especially as shortly after this the powerful religious inhibition of thought is brought into play by education. This is the type characterized by neurotic inhibition. We know very well that the intellectual weakness which has been acquired in this way gives an effective impetus to the outbreak of a neurotic illness. In a second type the intellectual development is sufficiently strong to resist the sexual repression which has hold of it. Some time after the infantile sexual researches have come to an end, the intelligence, having grown stronger, recalls the old association and offers its help in evading sexual repression, and the suppressed sexual activities of research return from the unconscious in the form of compulsive brooding, naturally in a distorted and unfree form, but sufficiently powerful to sexualize thinking itself and to colour intellectual operations with the pleasure and anxiety that belong to sexual processes proper. Here investigation becomes a sexual activity, often the exclusive one, and the feeling that comes from settling things in one's mind and explaining them replaces

[1] These improbable-sounding assertions can be confirmed from a study of my 'Analysis of a Phobia in a Five-Year-Old Boy' (1909b) and of similar observations. [Before 1924 these last words ran: 'and of the similar observation in Volume II of the Jahrbuch für psychonanalytische und psychopathologische Forschungen'—a reference to Jung (1910).] In a paper on 'The Sexual Theories of Children' (1908c) I wrote: 'This brooding and doubting, however, becomes the prototype of all later intellectual work directed towards the solution of problems, and the first failure has a crippling effect on the child's whole future.'

sexual satisfaction; but the interminable character of the child's researches is also repeated in the fact that this brooding never ends and that the intellectual feeling, so much desired, of having found a solution recedes more and more into the distance.

In virtue of a special disposition, the third type, which is the rarest and most perfect, escapes both inhibition of thought and neurotic compulsive thinking. It is true that here too sexual repression comes about, but it does not succeed in relegating a component instinct of sexual desire to the unconscious. Instead, the libido evades the fate of repression by being sublimated from the very beginning into curiosity and by becoming attached to the powerful instinct for research as a reinforcement. Here, too, the research becomes to some extent compulsive and a substitute for sexual activity; but owing to the complete difference in the underlying psychical processes (sublimation instead of an irruption from the unconscious) the quality of neurosis is absent; there is no attachment to the original complexes of infantile sexual research, and the instinct can operate freely in the service of intellectual interest. Sexual repression, which has made the instinct so strong through the addition to it of sublimated libido, is still taken into account by the instinct, in that it avoids any concern with sexual themes.

If we reflect on the concurrence in Leonardo of his overpowerful instinct for research and the atrophy of his sexual life (which was restricted to what is called ideal [sublimated] homosexuality) we shall be disposed to claim him as a model instance of our third type. The core of his nature, and the secret of it, would appear to be that after his curiosity had been activated in infancy in the service of sexual interests he succeeded in sublimating the greater part of his libido into an urge for research. But it is not easy, to be sure, to prove that this view is right. To do so we should need some picture of his mental development in the first years of his childhood, and it seems foolish to hope for material of that sort when the accounts of his life are so meagre and so unreliable, and when moreover it is a question of information about circumstances that escape the attention of observers even in relation to people of our own generation.

About Leonardo's youth we know very little. He was born in 1452 in the little town of Vinci between Florence and Empoli; he was an illegitimate child, which in those days was certainly not considered a grave social stigma; his father was Ser Piero da Vinci, a notary and descended from a family of notaries and farmers who took their name from the locality of Vinci; his mother was a certain Caterina, probably a peasant girl, who later married another native of Vinci. This mother does not occur again in the history of Leonardo's life, and it is only Merezhkovsky—the novelist—who believes that he has succeeded in finding some trace of her. The only definite piece of information about Leonardo's childhood comes in an official document of the year 1457; it is a Florentine land-register for the purpose of taxation, which mentions Leonardo among the members of the household of the Vinci family as the five-year-old illegitimate child of Ser Piero.[1] The marriage of Ser Piero with a certain Donna Albiera remained childless, and it was therefore possible for the young Leonardo to be brought up in his father's house. He did not leave this house till—at what age is not known—he entered Andrea del Verrocchio's studio as an apprentice. In the year 1472 Leonardo's name was already to be found in the list of members of the 'Compagnia dei Pittori'. That is all.

[1] Scognamiglio (1900, 15).

2

There is, so far as I know, only one place in his scientific note-books where Leonardo inserts a piece of information about his childhood. In a passage about the flight of vultures he suddenly interrupts himself to pursue a memory from very early years which had sprung to his mind:

'It seems that I was always destined to be so deeply concerned with vultures; for I recall as one of my very earliest memories that while I was in my cradle a vulture came down to mè, and opened my mouth with its tail, and struck me many times with its tail against my lips.'[1]

What we have here is a childhood memory; and certainly one

[1] 'Questo scriver si distintamente del nibio par che sia mio destino, perchè nella mia prima recordatione della mia infantia e' mi parea che, essendo io in culla, che un nibio venissi a me e mi aprissi la bocca colla sua coda e molte volte mi percuotesse con tal coda dentro alle labbra.' (Codex Atlanticus, F.65 v., as given by Scognamiglio [1900, 22].) [In the German text Frend quotes Herzfeld's translation of the Italian original, and our version above is a render-ing of the German. There are in fact two inaccuracies in the German: 'nibio' should be 'kite' not 'vulture' (See Editor's Note, p.5), and 'dentro', 'within', is omitted. This last omission is in fact rectified by Freud himself below (p. 35).]

of the strangest sort. It is strange on account of its content and on account of the age to which it is assigned. That a person should be able to retain a memory of his suckling period is perhaps not impossible, but it cannot by any means be regarded as certain. What, however, this memory of Leonardo's asserts—namely that a vulture opened the child's mouth with its tail—sounds so improbable, so fabulous, that another view of it, which at a single stroke puts an end to both difficulties, has more to commend it to our judgement. On this view the scene with the vulture would not be a memory of Leonardo's but a phantasy, which he formed at a later date and transposed to his childhood.[1]

This is often the way in which childhood memories originate. Quite unlike conscious memories from the time of maturity, they are not fixed at the moment of being experienced and afterwards repeated, but are only elicited at a later age when childhood is already past; in the process they are altered and falsified, and are put into the service of later trends, so that

---

[1] [*Footnote added* 1919:] In a friendly notice of this book Havelock Ellis (1910) has challenged the view put forward above. He objects that this memory of Leonardo's may very well have had a basis of reality, since children's memories often reach very much further back than is commonly supposed; the large bird in question need not of course have been a vulture. This is a point that I will gladly concede, and as a step towards lessening the difficulty I in turn will offer a suggestion—namely that his mother observed the large bird's visit to her child—an event which may easily have had the significance of an omen in her eyes—and repeatedly told him about it afterwards. As a result, I suggest, he retained the memory of his mother's story, and later, as so often happens, it became possible for him to take it for a memory of an experience of his own. However, this alteration does no damage to the force of my general account. It happens, indeed, as a general rule that the phantasies about their childhood which people construct at a late date are attached to trivial but real events of this early, and normally forgotten, period. There must thus have been some secret reason for bringing into prominence a real event of no importance and for elaborating it in the sort of way Leonardo did in his story of the bird, which he dubbed a vulture, and of its remarkable behaviour.

generally speaking they cannot be sharply distinguished from phantasies. Their nature is perhaps best illustrated by a comparison with the way in which the writing of history originated among the peoples of antiquity. As long as a nation was small and weak it gave no thought to the writing of its history. Men tilled the soil of their land, fought for their existence against their neighbours, and tried to gain territory from them and to acquire wealth. It was an age of heroes, not of historians. Then came another age, an age of reflection: men felt themselves to be rich and powerful, and now felt a need to learn where they had come from and how they had developed. Historical writing, which had begun to keep a continuous record of the present, now also cast a glance back to the past, gathered traditions and legends, interpreted the traces of antiquity that survived in customs and usages, and in this way created a history of the past. It was inevitable that this early history should have been an expression of present beliefs and wishes rather than a true picture of the past; for many things had been dropped from the nation's memory, while others were distorted, and some remains of the past were given a wrong interpretation in order to fit in with contemporary ideas. Moreover people's motive for writing history was not objective but a desire to influence their contemporaries, to encourage and inspire them, or to hold a mirror up before them. A man's conscious memory of the events of his maturity is in every way comparable to the first kind of historical writing [which was a chronicle of current events]; while the memories that he has of his childhood correspond, as far as their origins and reliability are concerned, to the history of a nation's earliest days, which was compiled later and for tendentious reasons.[1]

---

[1] [Chapter IV of The Psychopathology of Everyday Life (1901b) deals with childhood memories and screen-memories, and, in an addition made to it in 1907, Freud makes the same comparison with historical writing.]

If, then, Leonardo's story about the vulture that visited him in his cradle is only a phantasy from a later period, one might suppose it could hardly be worth while spending much time on it. One might be satisfied with explaining it on the basis of his inclination, of which he makes no secret, to regard his pre-occupation with the flight of birds as pre-ordained by destiny. Yet in underrating this story one would be committing just as great an injustice as if one were carelessly to reject the body of legends, traditions and interpretations found in a nation's early history. In spite of all the distortions and misunderstandings, they still represent the reality of the past: they are what a people forms out of the experience of its early days and under the dominance of motives that were once powerful and still operate to-day; and if it were only possible, by a knowledge of all the forces at work, to undo these distortions, there would be no difficulty in disclosing the historical truth lying behind the legendary material. The same holds good for the childhood memories or phantasies of an individual. What someone thinks he remembers from his childhood is not a matter of indiffer-ence; as a rule the residual memories—which he himself does not understand—cloak priceless pieces of evidence about the most important features in his mental development.[1] As we now

---

[1] [*Footnote added* 1919:] Since I wrote the above words I have attempted to make similar use of an unintelligible memory dating from the childhood of another man of genius. In the account of his life that Goethe wrote when he was about sixty ('*Dichtung und Wahrheit*') there is a description in the first few pages of how, with the encouragement of his neighbours, he slung first some small and then some large pieces of crockery out of the window into the street, so that they were smashed to pieces. This is, indeed, the only scene that he reports from the earliest years of childhood. The sheer inconsequentiality of its content, the way in which it corresponded with the childhood memories of other human beings who did not become particularly great, and the absence in this passage of any mention of the young brother who was born when Goethe was three and three-quarters, and who died when he was nearly ten—all this induced me to undertake an analysis of this childhood memory. (This child is in fact

possess in the techniques of psycho-analysis excellent methods for helping us to bring this concealed material to light, we may venture to fill in the gap in Leonardo's life story by analysing his childhood phantasy. And if in doing so we remain dissatisfied with the degree of certainty which we achieve, we shall have to console ourselves with the reflection that so many other studies of this great and enigmatic man have met with no better fate.

If we examine with the eyes of a psycho-analyst Leonardo's phantasy of the vulture, it does not appear strange for long. We seem to recall having come across the same sort of thing in many places, for example in dreams; so that we may venture to translate the phantasy from its own special language into words that are generally understood. The translation is then seen to point to an erotic content. A tail, 'coda', is one of the most familiar symbols and substitutive expressions for the male organ, in Italian no less than in other languages;[1] the situation in the phantasy, of

mentioned at a later point in the book, where Goethe dwells on the many illnesses of childhood.) I hoped to be able as a result to replace it by something which would be more in keeping with the context of Goethe's account and whose content would make it worthy of preservation and of the place he has given it in the history of his life. The short analysis ['A Childhood Recollection from *Dichtung und Wahrheit*' (1917b)] made it possible for the throwing-out of the crockery to be recognized as a magical act directed against a troublesome intruder; and at the place in the book where he describes the episode the intention is to triumph over the fact that a second son was not in the long run permitted to disturb Goethe's close relation with his mother. If the earliest memory of childhood, preserved in disguises such as these, should be concerned—in Goethe's case as well as in Leonardo's—with the mother, what would be so surprising in that?—[In the 1919 edition the phrase 'and the absence in this passage of any mention of the young brother . . .' ran ' . . . and the remarkable absence of any mention whatever of a young brother . . . ' It was given its present form, and the parenthesis that follows it was added, in 1923. The alteration is explained in a footnote added in 1924 to the Goethe paper (1917b), *Standard Ed.*, **17**, 151n.]

[1] [Cf. the 'Original Record' of the case of the 'Rat Man', *Standard Ed.*, **10**, 311.— It may be pointed out (supposing the bird to have been in fact a kite) that the

a vulture opening the child's mouth and beating about inside it[1] vigorously with its tail, corresponds to the idea of an act of *fellatio*, a sexual act in which the penis is put into the mouth of the person involved. It is strange that this phantasy is so completely passive in character; moreover it resembles certain dreams and phantasies found in women or passive homosexuals (who play the part of the woman in sexual relations).

I hope the reader will restrain himself and not allow a surge of indignation to prevent his following psycho-analysis any further because it leads to an unpardonable aspersion on the memory of a great and pure man the very first time it is applied to his case. Such indignation, it is clear, will never be able to tell us the significance of Leonardo's childhood phantasy; at the same time Leonardo has acknowledged the phantasy in the most unambiguous fashion, and we cannot abandon our expectation—or, if it sounds better, our prejudice—that a phantasy of this kind must have *some* meaning, in the same way as any other psychical creation: a dream, a vision or a delirium. Let us rather therefore give a fair hearing for a while to the work of analysis, which indeed has not yet spoken its last word.

The inclination to take a man's sexual organ into the mouth and suck at it, which in respectable society is considered a loathsome sexual perversion, is nevertheless found with great frequency among women of to-day—and of earlier times as well, as ancient sculptures show—, and in the state of being in love it appears completely to lose its repulsive character. Phantasies derived from this inclination are found by doctors even in

kite's long forked tail is one of its noticeable features and plays a large part in the virtuosity of its movements in the air and no doubt attracted Leonardo's attention in his observations of flight. The symbolic meaning of its *coda*, discussed by Freud in this passage, seems to be confirmed by a remark in an ornithological account of the kite published recently in *The Times* (July 7, 1956): 'At times the tail is fanned out at right angles to its normal plane.']

[1] [See end of footnote on p. 30.]

women who have not become aware of the possibilities of obtaining sexual satisfaction in this way by reading Krafft-Ebing's *Psychopathia Sexualis* or from other sources of information. Women, it seems, find no difficulty in producing this kind of wishful phantasy spontaneously.[1] Further investigation informs us that this situation, which morality condemns with such severity, may be traced to an origin of the most innocent kind. It only repeats in a different form a situation in which we all once felt comfortable—when we were still in our suckling days ('*essendo io in culla*')[2] and took our mother's (or wet-nurse's) nipple into our mouth and sucked at it. The organic impression of this experience—the first source of pleasure in our life—doubtless remains indelibly printed on us; and when at a later date the child becomes familiar with the cow's udder whose function is that of a nipple, but whose shape and position under the belly make it resemble a penis, the preliminary stage has been reached which will later enable him to form the repellent sexual phantasy.[3]

Now we understand why Leonardo assigned the memory of his supposed experiment with the vulture to his suckling period. What the phantasy conceals is merely a reminiscence of sucking—or being suckled—at his mother's breast, a scene of human beauty that he, like so many artists, undertook to depict with his brush, in the guise of the mother of God and her child. There is indeed another point which we do not yet understand and which we must not lose sight of: this reminiscence, which has the same importance for both sexes, has been transformed by the man Leonardo into a passive homosexual phantasy. For the time being we shall put aside the question of what there may

---

[1] On this point compare my 'Fragment of an Analysis of a Case of Hysteria' (1905e) [*Standard Ed.*, **7**, 51].

[2] ['While I was in my cradle.' See footnote 1, p. 30 above.]

[3] [Cf. the analysis of 'Little Hans', *Standard Ed.*, **10**, 7.]

be to connect homosexuality with the sucking at the mother's breast, merely recalling that tradition does in fact represent Leonardo as a man with homosexual feelings. In this connection, it is irrelevant to our purpose whether the charge brought against the young Leonardo [p. 18] was justified or not. What decides whether we describe someone as an invert[1] is not his actual behaviour, but his emotional attitude.

Our interest is next claimed by another unintelligible feature of Leonardo's childhood phantasy. We interpret the phantasy as one of being suckled by his mother, and we find his mother replaced by—a vulture. Where does this vulture come from and how does it happen to be found in its present place?

At this point a thought comes to the mind from such a remote quarter that it would be tempting to set it aside. In the hieroglyphics of the ancient Egyptians the mother is represented by a picture of a vulture.[2] The Egyptians also worshipped a Mother Goddess, who was represented as having a vulture's head, or else several heads, of which at least one was a vulture's.[3] This goddess's name was pronounced Mut. Can the similarity to the sound of our word Mutter ['mother'] be merely a coincidence? There is, then, some real connection between vulture and mother—but what help is that to us? For have we any right to expect Leonardo to know of it, seeing that the first man who succeeded in reading hieroglyphics was François Champollion (1790–1832)?[4]

It would be interesting to enquire how it could be that the ancient Egyptians came to choose the vulture as a symbol of motherhood. Now the religion and civilization of the Egyptians were objects of scientific curiosity even to the Greeks and the

[1] [In 1910 only: 'a homosexual'.]
[2] Horapollo (Hieroglyphica **1**, 11): 'Μητέρα δὲ γράφοντες ... γῦπα ζωγραφοῦσιν.' ['To denote a mother ... they delineate a vulture.']
[3] Roscher (1894–97), Lanzone (1882).
[4] Hartleben (1906).

Romans: and long before we ourselves were able to read the
monuments of Egypt we had at our disposal certain pieces of
information about them derived from the extant writings of
classical antiquity. Some of these writings were by well-known
authors, such as Strabo, Plutarch and Ammianus Marcellinus;
while others bear unfamiliar names and are uncertain in their
source of origin and their date of composition, like the *Hieroglyphica* of Horapollo Nilous and the book of oriental priestly
wisdom which has come down to us under the name of the god
Hermes Trismegistos. We learn from these sources that the vulture was regarded as a symbol of motherhood because only
female vultures were believed to exist; there were, it was thought,
no males of this species.[1] A counterpart to this restriction to one
sex was also known to the natural history of antiquity: in the
case of the scarabaeus beetle, which the Egyptians worshipped as
divine, it was thought that only males existed.[2]

How then were vultures supposed to be impregnated if all of
them were female? This is a point fully explained in a passage in
Horapollo.[3] At a certain time these birds pause in mid-flight,
open their vagina and are impregnated by the wind.

---

[1] 'γῦπα δὲ ἄρρενα ὅυ φασι γινέσθαι ποτε, ἀλλὰ θηλείας ἁπάσας.' ['They say
that no male vulture has ever existed but all are females.' Aelian, *De Natura
Animalium*, II, 46.] Quoted by von Römer (1903, 732).

[2] Plutarch: 'Veluti scarabaeos mares tantum esse putarunt Aegyptii sic inter
vultures mares non inveniri statuerunt.' ['Just as they believed that only male
scarabs existed, so the Egyptians concluded that no male vultures were to be
found.' Freud has here inadvertently attributed to Plutarch a sentence which is
in fact a gloss by Leemans (1835, 171) on Horapollo.]

[3] *Horapollonis Niloi Hieroglyphica*, ed. Leemans (1835, 14). The words that refer to
the vulture's sex run: 'μητέρα μέν, ἐπειδὴ ἄρρεν ἐν τούτωτψ τῷ γένει τῶν
ζώων οὐχ ὑπάρχει.' ['(They use the picture of a vulture to denote) a mother,
because in this race of creatures there are no males.'—It seems as though the
wrong passage from Horapollo is quoted here. The phrase in the text implies
that what we should have here is the myth of the vulture's impregnation by the
wind.]

We have now unexpectedly reached a position where we can take something as very probable which only a short time before we had to reject as absurd. It is quite possible that Leonardo was familiar with the scientific fable which was responsible for the vulture being used by the Egyptians as a pictorial representation of the idea of mother. He was a wide reader and his interest embraced all branches of literature and learning. In the Codex Atlanticus we find a catalogue of all the books he possessed at a particular date,[1] and in addition numerous jottings on other books that he had borrowed from friends; and if we may judge by the extracts from his notes by Richter [1883],[2] the extent of his reading can hardly be overestimated. Early works on natural history were well represented among them in addition to contemporary books; and all of them were already in print at the time. Milan was in fact the leading city in Italy for the new art of printing.

On proceeding further we come across a piece of information which can turn the probability that Leonardo knew the fable of the vulture into a certainty. The learned editor and commentator on Horapollo has the following note on the text already quoted above [Leemans, 1835, 172]: 'Caeterum hanc fabulam de vulturibus cupide amplexi sunt Patres Ecclesiastici, ut ita argumento ex rerum natura petito refutarent eos, qui Virginis partum negabant; itaque apud omnes fere hujus rei mentio occurrit.'[3]

So the fable of the single sex of vultures and their mode of conception remained something very far from an unimportant anecdote like the analogous tale of the scarabaeus beetle; it had been seized on by the Fathers of the Church so that they could

[1] Müntz (1899, 282).

[2] Müntz (ibid.).

[3] ['But this story about the vulture was eagerly taken up by the Fathers of the Church, in order to refute, by means of a proof drawn from the natural order, those who denied the Virgin Birth. The subject is therefore mentioned in almost all of them.']

have at their disposal a proof drawn from natural history to confront those who doubted sacred history. If vultures were described in the best accounts of antiquity as depending on the wind for impregnation, why could not the same thing have also happened on one occasion with a human female? Since the fable of the vulture could be turned to this account 'almost all' the Fathers of the Church made a practice of telling it, and thus it can hardly be doubted that Leonardo too came to know of it through its being favoured by so wide a patronage.

We can now reconstruct the origin of Leonardo's vulture phantasy. He once happened to read in one of the Fathers or in a book on natural history the statement that all vultures were females and could reproduce their kind without any assistance from a male: and at that point a memory sprang to his mind, which was transformed into the phantasy we have been discussing, but which meant to signify that he also had been such a vulture-child—he had had a mother, but no father. With this memory was associated, in the only way in which impressions of so great an age can find expression, an echo of the pleasure he had had at his mother's breast. The allusion made by the Fathers of the Church to the idea of the Blessed Virgin and her child—an idea cherished by every artist—must have played its part in helping the phantasy to appear valuable and important to him. Indeed in this way he was able to identify himself with the child Christ, the comforter and saviour not of this one woman alone.

Our aim in dissecting a childhood phantasy is to separate the real memory that it contains from the later motives that modify and distort it. In Leonardo's case we believe that we now know the real content of the phantasy: the replacement of his mother by the vulture indicates that the child was aware of his father's absence and found himself alone with his mother. The fact of Leonardo's illegitimate birth is in harmony with his vulture phantasy; it was only on this account that he could compare himself to a vulture child. But the next reliable fact that we possess about his youth is that by the time he was five he had been received into his father's household. We are completely ignorant when that happened—whether it was a few months after his birth or whether it was a few weeks before the drawing-up of the land-register [p. 29]. It is here that the interpretation of the vulture phantasy comes in: Leonardo, it seems to tell us, spent the critical first years of his life not by the side of his father and stepmother, but with his poor, forsaken, real mother, so that he had time to feel the absence of his father. This seems a slender and yet a somewhat daring conclusion to have emerged from our psycho-analytic efforts, but its significance will increase as we continue our investigation. Its certainty is reinforced when we consider the circumstances that did in fact operate in Leonardo's childhood. In the same year that Leonardo was born, the sources tell us, his father, Ser Piero da Vinci, married Donna Albiera, a lady of good birth; it was to the childlessness of this marriage that the boy owed his reception into his father's (or rather his grandfather's) house—an event which had taken place by the time he was five years old, as the document attests. Now it is not usual at the start of a marriage to put an illegitimate offspring into the care of the young bride who still expects to be blessed with children of her own. Years of disappointment must surely first have elapsed before it was decided to adopt the illegitimate child—who had probably grown up an attractive young boy—as a compensation for the absence of the legiti-mate children that had been hoped for. It fits in best with the interpretation of the vulture phantasy if at least three years of Leonardo's life, and perhaps five, had elapsed before he could exchange the solitary person of his mother for a parental couple. And by then it was too late. In the first three or four years of life certain impressions become fixed and ways of reacting to the outside world are established which can never be deprived of their importance by later experiences.

If it is true that the unintelligible memories of a person's childhood and the phantasies that are built on them invariably emphasize the most important elements in his mental development, then it follows that the fact which the vulture fantasy confirms, namely that Leonardo spent the first years of his life alone with his mother, will have been of decisive influence in the formation of his inner life. An inevitable effect of this state of affairs was that the child—who was confronted in his early life with one problem more than other children—began to brood on this riddle with special intensity, and so at a tender age became a researcher, tormented as he was by the great question of where babies come from and what the father has to do with their origin.[1] It was a vague suspicion that his researches and the history of his childhood were connected in this way which later prompted him to exclaim that he had been destined from the first to investigate the problem of the flight of birds since he had been visited by a vulture as he lay in his cradle. Later on it will not be difficult to show how his curiosity about the flight of birds was derived from the sexual researches of his childhood.

[1] [Cf. 'The Sexual Theories of Children' (1908c).]

3

In Leonardo's childhood phantasy we have taken the element of the vulture to represent the real content of his memory, while the context in which Leonardo himself placed his phantasy has thrown a bright light on the importance which that content had for his later life. In proceeding with our work of interpretation we now come up against the strange problem of why this content has been recast into a homosexual situation. The mother who suckles her child—or to put it better, at whose breast the child sucks—has been turned into a vulture that puts its tail into the child's mouth. We have asserted [p. 34] that, according to the usual way in which language makes use of substitutes, the vulture's 'coda' cannot possibly signify anything other than a male genital, a penis. But we do not understand how imaginative activity can have succeeded in endowing precisely this bird which is a mother with the distinguishing mark of masculinity; and in view of this absurdity we are at a loss how to reduce this creation of Leonardo's phantasy to any rational meaning.

However, we should not despair, as we reflect on the number of apparently absurd dreams that we have in the past compelled to give up their meaning. Is there any reason why a memory of childhood should offer us more difficulty than a dream?

Remembering that it is unsatisfactory when a peculiar feature is found singly, let us hasten to add another to it which is even more striking.[1]

The vulture-headed Egyptian goddess Mut, a figure without any personal character according to Drexler's article in Roscher's lexicon, was often merged with other mother goddesses of a more strongly marked individuality, like Isis and Hathor, but at the same time she maintained her separate existence and cult. A special feature of the Egyptian pantheon was that the individual gods did not disappear in the process of syncretization. Alongside the fusion of gods the individual divinities continued to exist in independence. Now this vulture-headed mother goddess was usually represented by the Egyptians with a phallus;[2] her body was female, as the breasts indicated, but it also had a male organ in a state of erection.

In the goddess Mut, then, we find the same combination of maternal and masculine characteristics as in Leonardo's phantasy of the vulture. Are we to explain this coincidence by assuming that from studying his books [cf. p. 39] Leonardo had also learnt of the androgynous nature of the maternal vulture? Such a possibility is more than questionable; it appears that the sources to which he had access contained no information about this remarkable feature. It is more plausible to trace the correspondence back to a common factor operative in both cases but still unknown.

Mythology can teach us that an androgynous structure, a combination of male and female sex characters, was an attribute not only of Mut but also of other deities like Isis and Hathor—

[1] [Cf. some similar remarks by Freud in *The Interpretation of Dreams* (1900a), Standard Ed., **4**, 135–6.]

[2] See the illustrations in Lanzone (1882, Plates CXXXVI-CXXXVIII).

though perhaps of these only in so far as they too had a maternal nature and became amalgamated with Mut (Römer, 1903). It teaches us further that other Egyptian deities, like Neith of Sais—from whom the Greek Athene was later derived—were originally conceived of as androgynous, i.e. as hermaphrodite, and that the same was true of many of the Greek gods, especially of those associated with Dionysus, but also of Aphrodite, who was later restricted to the role of a female goddess of love. Mythology may then offer the explanation that the addition of a phallus to the female body is intended to denote the primal creative force of nature, and that all these hermaphrodite divinities are expressions of the idea that only a combination of male and female elements can give a worthy representation of divine perfection. But none of these considerations gives us an explanation of the puzzling psychological fact that human imagination does not boggle at endowing a figure which is intended to embody the essence of the mother with the mark of male potency which is the opposite of everything maternal.

Infantile sexual theories provide the explanation. There was once a time when the male genital was found compatible with the picture of the mother.[1] When a male child first turns his curiosity to the riddles of sexual life, he is dominated by his interest in his own genital. He finds that part of his body too valuable and too important for him to be able to believe that it could be missing in other people whom he feels he resembles so much. As he cannot guess that there exists another type of genital structure of equal worth, he is forced to make the assumption that all human beings, women as well as men, possess a penis like his own. This preconception is so firmly planted in the youthful investigator that it is not destroyed even when he first observes the genitals of little girls. His perception tells him, it is true, that there is something different from what there is in him,

[1] [Cf. 'The Sexual Theories of Children' (1908c).]

but he is incapable of admitting to himself that the content of this perception is that he cannot find a penis in girls. That the penis could be missing strikes him as an uncanny and intolerable idea, and so in an attempt at a compromise he comes to the conclusion that little girls have a penis as well, only it is still very small; it will grow later.[1] If it seems from later observations that this expectation is not realized, he has another remedy at his disposal: little girls too had a penis, but it was cut off and in its place was left a wound. This theoretical advance already makes use of personal experiences of a distressing kind: the boy in the meantime has heard the threat that the organ which is so dear to him will be taken away from him if he shows his interest in it too plainly. Under the influence of this threat of castration he now sees the notion he has gained of the female genitals in a new light; henceforth he will tremble for his masculinity, but at the same time he will despise the unhappy creatures on whom the cruel punishment has, as he supposes, already fallen.[2]

Before the child comes under the dominance of the castration-complex—at a time when he still holds women at full value—he begins to display an intense desire to look, as an erotic instinctual activity. He wants to see other people's genitals, at first in all probability to compare them with his own. The erotic

[1] Compare the observations in the *Jahrbuch für psychoanalytische und psychopathologische Forschungen* [i.e. Freud, 1909b ('Little Hans'), *Standard Ed.*, **10**, 11, and Jung, 1910.—*Added* 1919:], in the *Internationale Zeitschrift für ärztliche Psychoanalyse* and in [the section dealing with children in] *Imago*.

[2] [*Footnote added* 1919:] The conclusion strikes me as inescapable that here we may also trace one of the roots of the anti-semitism which appears with such elemental force and finds such irrational expression among the nations of the West. Circumcision is unconsciously equated with castration. If we venture to carry our conjectures back to the primaeval days of the human race we can surmise that originally circumcision must have been a milder substitute, designed to take the place of castration. [Further discussion on this will be found in a footnote to the analysis of 'Little Hans' (1909b) *Standard Ed.*, **10**, 36, and in *Moses and Monotheism* (1939a), Chapter III, Part I, Section D.]

attraction that comes from his mother soon culminates in a longing for her genital organ, which he takes to be a penis. With the discovery, which is not made till later, that women do not have a penis, this longing often turns into its opposite and gives place to a feeling of disgust which in the years of puberty can become the cause of psychical impotence, misogyny and permanent homosexuality. But the fixation on the object that was once strongly desired, the woman's penis, leaves indelible traces on the mental life of the child, who has pursued that portion of his infantile sexual researches with particular thoroughness. Fetishistic reverence for a woman's foot and shoe appears to take the foot merely as a substitutive symbol for the woman's penis which was once revered and later missed; without knowing it, '*coupeurs de nattes*'[1] play the part of people who carry out an act of castration on the female genital organ.

People will not reach a proper understanding of the activities of children's sexuality and will probably take refuge in declaring that what has been said here is incredible, so long as they cling to the attitude taken up by our civilization of depreciating the genitals and the sexual functions. To understand the mental life of children we require analogies from primitive times. Through a long series of generations the genitals have been for us the '*pudenda*', objects of shame, and even (as a result of further successful sexual repression) of disgust. If one makes a broad survey of the sexual life of our time and in particular of the classes who sustain human civilization, one is tempted to declare that[2] it is only with reluctance that the majority of those alive to-day obey the command to propagate their kind; they feel that their dignity as human beings suffers and is degraded in the process. What is to be found among us in the way of another view of sexual life is confined to the uncultivated lower strata of society; among the

---

[1] [Perverts who enjoy cutting off females' hair.]

[2] [The sentence up to this point was added in 1919.]

higher and more refined classes it is concealed, since it is considered culturally inferior, and it ventures to put itself into practice only in the face of a bad conscience. In the primaeval days of
the human race it was a different story. The laborious compil-
ations of the student of civilization provide convincing evidence
that originally the genitals were the pride and hope of living
beings; they were worshipped as gods and transmitted the divine nature of their functions to all newly learned human activities. As a result of the sublimation of their basic nature there
arose innumerable divinities; and at the time when the connection between official religions and sexual activity was already
hidden from the general consciousness, secret cults devoted
themselves to keeping it alive among a number of initiates. In
the course of cultural development so much of the divine and
sacred was ultimately extracted from sexuality that the
exhausted remnant fell into contempt. But in view of the indeli-
bility that is characteristic of all mental traces, it is surely not
surprising that even the most primitive forms of genital-
worship can be shown to have existed in very recent times
and that the language, customs and superstitions of mankind
to-day contain survivals from every phase of this process of
development.[1]

Impressive analogies from biology have prepared us to find
that the individual's mental development repeats the course of
human development in an abbreviated form; and the conclusions which psycho-analytic research into the child's mind has
reached concerning the high value set on the genitals in infancy
will not therefore strike us as improbable. The child's assumption that his mother has a penis is thus the common source from
which are derived the androgynously-formed mother goddesses
such as the Egyptian Mut and the vultures' 'coda' in Leonardo's
childhood phantasy. It is in fact only due to a misunderstanding

[1] Cf. Knight [1768].

that we describe these representations of gods as hermaphrodite in the medical sense of the word. In none of them is there a combination of the true genitals of both sexes—a combination which, to the abhorrence of all beholders, is found in some cases of malformation; all that has happened is that the male organ has been added to the breasts which are the mark of a mother, just as it was present in the child's first idea of his mother's body. This form of the mother's body, the revered creation of primaeval phantasy, has been preserved for the faithful by mythology. We can now provide the following translation of the emphasis given to the vulture's tail in Leonardo's phantasy: 'That was a time when my fond curiosity was directed to my mother, and when I still believed she had a genital organ like my own.' Here is more evidence of Leonardo's early sexual researches, which in our opinion had a decisive effect on the whole of his later life.

At this point a little reflection will remind us that we ought not to feel satisfied yet with the way the vulture's tail in Leonardo's childhood phantasy has been explained. Something more seems to be contained in it which we do not yet understand. Its most striking feature, after all, was that it changed sucking at the mother's breast into being suckled, that is, into passivity, and thus into a situation whose nature is undoubtedly homosexual. When we remember the historical probability of Leonardo having behaved in his life as one who was emotionally homosexual, the question is forced upon us whether this phantasy does not indicate the existence of a causal connection between Leonardo's relation with his mother in childhood and his later manifest, if ideal [sublimated], homosexuality. We should not venture to infer a connection of this sort from Leonardo's distorted reminiscence if we did not know from the psycho-analytic study of homosexual patients that such a connection does exist and is in fact an intimate and necessary one.

Homosexual men, who have in our times taken vigorous action against the restrictions imposed by law on their sexual activity, are fond of representing themselves, through their theoretical spokesmen, as being from the outset a distinct sexual species, as an intermediate sexual stage, as a 'third sex'. They are, they claim, men who are innately compelled by organic determinants to find pleasure in men and have been debarred from obtaining it in women. Much as one would be glad on grounds of humanity to endorse their claims, one must treat their theories with some reserve, for they have been advanced without regard for the psychical genesis of homosexuality. Psycho-analysis offers the means of filling this gap and of putting the assertions of homosexuals to the test. It has succeeded in the task only in the case of a small number of persons, but all the investigations undertaken so far have yielded the same surprising result.[1] In all our male homosexual cases the subjects had had a very intense erotic attachment to a female person, as a rule their mother, during the first period of childhood, which is afterwards forgotten; this attachment was evoked or encouraged by too much tenderness on the part of the mother herself, and further reinforced by the small part played by the father during their childhood. Sadger emphasizes the fact that the mothers of his homosexual patients were frequently masculine women, women with energetic traits of character, who were able to push the father out of his proper place. I have occasionally seen the same thing, but I was more strongly impressed by cases in which the father was absent from the beginning or left the scene at an early date, so that the boy found himself left entirely under feminine influence. Indeed it almost seems as though the presence of a strong father would ensure that the son made the

[1] I refer in particular to the investigations of I. Sadger, which I can in the main confirm from my own experience. I am also aware that Wilhelm Stekel of Vienna and Sándor Ferenci of Budapest have arrived at the same results.

correct decision in his choice of object, namely someone of the opposite sex.[1]

After this preliminary stage a transformation sets in whose mechanism is known to us but whose motive forces we do not yet understand. The child's love for his mother cannot continue to develop consciously any further; it succumbs to repression. The boy represses his love for his mother: he puts himself in her place, identifies himself with her, and takes his own person as a model in whose likeness he chooses the new objects of his love. In this way he has become a homosexual. What he has in fact done is to slip back to auto-erotism: for the boys whom he now loves as he grows up are after all only substitutive figures and revivals of himself in childhood—boys whom he loves in the way in which his mother loved him when he was a child. He finds the objects of his love along the path of *narcissism*, as we say; for Narcissus, according to the Greek legend, was a youth who preferred his own reflection to everything else and who was changed into the lovely flower of that name.[2]

[1] [*Footnote added* 1919:] Psycho-analytic research has contributed two facts that are beyond question to the understanding of homosexuality, without at the same time supposing that it has exhausted the causes of this sexual aberration. The first is the fixation of the erotic needs on the mother which has been mentioned above; the other is contained in the statement that everyone, even the most normal person, is capable of making a homosexual object-choice, and has done so at some time in his life, and either still adheres to it in his unconscious or else protects himself against it by vigorous counter-attitudes. These two discoveries put an end both to the claim of homosexuals to be regarded as a 'third sex' and to what has been believed to be the important distinction between innate and acquired homosexuality. The presence of somatic characters of the other sex (the quota provided by physical herm-aphroditism) is highly conductive to the homosexual object-choice becoming manifest; but it is not derisive. It must be stated with regret that those who speak for the homosexuals in the field of science have been incapable of learning anything from the established findings of psycho-analysis.

[2] [Freud's first published reference to narcissism had appeared only a few months before, in a footnote added to the second edition of his *Three Essays*

Psychological considerations of a deeper kind justify the assertion that a man who has become a homosexual in this way remains unconsciously fixated to the mnemic image of his mother. By repressing his love for his mother he preserves it in his unconscious and from now on remains faithful to her. While he seems to pursue boys and to be their lover, he is in reality running away from the other women, who might cause him to be unfaithful. In individual cases direct observation has also enabled us to show that the man who gives the appearance of being susceptible only to the charms of men is in fact attracted by women in the same way as a normal man; but on each occasion he hastens to transfer the excitation he has received from women on to a male object, and in this manner he repeats over and over again the mechanism by which he acquired his homosexuality.

We are far from wishing to exaggerate the importance of these explanations of the psychical genesis of homosexuality. It is quite obvious that they are in sharp contrast to the official theories of those who speak for homosexuals, but we know that they are not sufficiently comprehensive to make a conclusive explanation of the problem possible. What is for practical reasons called homosexuality may arise from a whole variety of psychosexual inhibitory processes; the particular process we have singled out is perhaps only one among many, and is perhaps related to only one type of 'homosexuality'. We must also admit that the number of cases of our homosexual type in which it is possible to point to the determinants which we require far exceeds the number of those where the deduced effect actually takes place; so that we too cannot reject the part

(1905d), *Standard Ed.*, **7**, 145n., which was published early in 1910. He had mentioned the concept at a meeting of the Vienna Psycho-Analytical Society on November 10, 1909. For a full-length discussion of the subject see 'On Narcissism: an Introduction' (1914c).]

played by unknown constitutional factors, to which the whole of homosexuality is usually traced. We should not have had any cause at all for entering into the psychical genesis of the form of homosexuality we have studied if there were not a strong presumption that Leonardo, whose phantasy of the vulture was our starting point, was himself a homosexual of this very type.[1]

Few details are known about the sexual behaviour of the great artist and scientist, but we may place confidence in the probability that the assertions of his contemporaries were not grossly erroneous. In the light of these traditions, then, he appears as a man whose sexual need and activity were exceptionally reduced, as if a higher aspiration had raised him above the common animal need of mankind. It may remain open to doubt whether he ever sought direct sexual satisfaction—and if so, in what manner—or whether he was able to dispense with it altogether. We are however justified in looking in him too for the emotional currents which drive other men imperatively on to perform the sexual act; for we cannot imagine the mental life of any human being in the formation of which sexual desire in the broadest sense—libido—did not have its share, even if that desire has departed far from its original aim, or has refrained from putting itself into effect.

We cannot expect to find in Leonardo anything more than *traces* of untransformed sexual inclination. But these point in one direction and moreover allow him to be reckoned as a homosexual. It has always been emphasized that he took only strikingly handsome boys and youths as pupils. He treated them with

---

[1] [A more general discussion of homosexuality and its genesis will be found in the first of Freud's *Three Essays* (1950d), particularly in a long footnote added between 1910 and 1920, *Standard Ed.*, **7**, 144–7. Among other, later, discussions of the subject may be mentioned his case history of a female homosexual (1920a) and 'Some Neurotic Mechanisms in Jealousy, Paranoia and Homosexuality' (1922b).]

kindness and consideration, looked after them, and when they were ill nursed them himself, just as a mother nurses her children and just as his own mother might have tended him. As he had chosen them for their beauty and not for their talent, none of them—Cesare da Sesto, Boltraffio, Andrea Salaino, Francesco Melzi and others—became a painter of importance. Generally they were unable to make themselves independent of their master, and after his death they disappeared without having left any definite mark on the history of art. The others, whose works entitled them to be called his pupils, like Luini and Bazi, called Sodoma, he probably did not know personally.

We realize that we shall have to meet the objection that Leonardo's behaviour towards his pupils has nothing at all to do with sexual motives and that it allows no conclusions to be drawn about his particular sexual inclination. Against this we wish to submit with all caution that our view explains some peculiar features of the artist's behaviour which would otherwise have to remain a mystery. Leonardo kept a diary; he made entries in his small hand (written from right to left) which were meant only for himself. It is noteworthy that in his diary he addressed himself in the second person. 'Learn the multiplication of roots from Master Luca.' (Solmi, 1908, 152). 'Get Master d'Abacco to show you how to square the circle.' (Loc. cit.) Or on the occasion of a journey: 'I am going to Milan on business to do with my garden . . . Have two baggage trunks made. Get Boltraffio to show you the turning-lathe and get him to polish a stone on it. Leave the book for Master Andrea il Todesco.' (Ibid., 203.)[1] Or a resolution of very different importance: 'You have to show in your treatise that the earth is a star, like the moon or something like it,

---

[1] Leonardo is behaving here like someone whose habit it was to make his daily confession to another person and who uses his diary as a substitute for him. For a conjecture as to who this person may have been, see Merezhkovsky (1903, 367).

and thus prove the nobility of our world.' (Herzfeld, 1906, 141.)

In this diary, which, by the way, like the diaries of other mortals, often dismisses the most important events of the day in a few words or else passes them over in complete silence, there are some entries which on account of their strangeness are quoted by all Leonardo's biographers. They are notes of small sums of money spent by the artist—notes recorded with a minute exactness, as if they were made by a pedantically strict and parsimonious head of a household. There is on the other hand no record of the expenditure of larger sums or any other evidence that the artist was at home in keeping accounts. One of these notes has to do with a new cloak which he bought for his pupil Andrea Salaino:[1]

Silver brocade	15	lire	4	soldi
Crimson velvet for trimming	9	,,	—	,,
Braid	—	,,	9	,,
Buttons	—	,,	12	,,

Another very detailed note brings together all the expenses he incurred through the bad character and thievish habits of another pupil:[2] 'On the twenty-first day of April, 1490, I began this book and made a new start on the horse.[3] Jacomo came to me on St. Mary Magdalen's day, 1490: he is ten years old.' (Marginal note: 'thievish, untruthful, selfish, greedy.') 'On the second day I had two shirts cut out for him, a pair of trousers and a jacket, and when I put the money aside to pay for these things, he stole the money from my purse, and it was never possible to make him own up, although I was absolutely sure of

---

[1] The text is that given by Merezhkovsky (1903, 282).

[2] Or model.

[3] For the equestrian statue of Francesco Sforza.

it.' (Marginal note: '4 lire . . .') The report of the child's mis-
deeds runs on in this way and ends with the reckoning of
expenses: 'In the first year, a cloak, 2 lire; 6 shirts, 4 lire; 3
jackets, 6 lire; 4 pairs of stockings, 7 lire; etc.'[1]

Nothing is further from the wishes of Leonardo's biographers
than to try to solve the problems in their hero's mental life by
starting from his small weaknesses and peculiarities; and the
usual comment that they make on these singular accounts is one
which lays stress on the artist's kindness and consideration for
his pupils. They forget that what calls for explanation is not
Leonardo's behaviour, but the fact that he left these pieces of
evidence of it behind him. As it is impossible to believe that his
motive was that of letting proofs of his good nature fall into our
hands, we must assume that it was another motive, an affective
one, which led him to write these notes down. What motive it
was is not easy to guess, and we should be unable to suggest one
if there were not another account found among Leonardo's
papers which throws a vivid light on these strangely trifling
notes about his pupils' clothing, etc.:

Expenses after Caterina's death for her funeral	27	florins
2 pounds of wax	18	,,
For transporting and erecting the cross	12	,,
Catafalque	4	,,
Pall-bearers	8	,,
For 4 priests and 4 clerks	20	,,
Bell-ringing	2	,,
For the grave-diggers	16	,,
For the licence—to the officials	1	,,
Total	108	florins.

---

[1] The full text is to be found in Herzfeld (1906, 45).

Previous expenses

    For the doctor   4 florins

    For sugar and candles 12   ,,

                                16 florins

                Grand total   124 florins.[1]

The novelist Merezhkovsky alone is able to tell us who this Caterina was. From two other short notes[2] he concludes that Leonardo's mother, the poor peasant woman of Vinci, came to Milan in 1493 to visit her son, who was then 41; that she fell ill there, was taken to hospital by Leonardo, and when she died was honoured by him with this costly funeral.

This interpretation by the psychological novelist cannot be put to the proof, but it can claim so much inner probability, and is so much in harmony with all that we otherwise know of Leonardo's emotional activity, that I cannot refrain from accepting it as correct. He had succeeded in subjecting his feelings to the yoke of research and in inhibiting their free utterance; but

---

[1] Merezbkovsky (1903, 372).—As a melancholy example of the uncertainty that surrounds the information, which is in any case scanty enough, about Leonardo's private life, I may mention the fact that the same account is quoted by Solmi (1908, 104) with considerable variations. The most serious one is that soldi are given instead of florins. It may be assumed that florins in this account do not mean the old 'gold florins' but the monetary units which were used later and were worth $1\frac{2}{3}$ lire or $33\frac{1}{3}$ soldi. Solmi makes Caterina a servant who had looked after Leonardo's household for some time. The source from which the two versions of these accounts were taken was not accessible to me. [The figures given actually vary to some extent in the different editions of Freud's own book. The cost of the catafalque is given in 1910 as '12', in 1919 and 1923 as '19' and from 1925 as '4'. Before 1925 the cost of transporting and erecting the cross was given as '4'. For a recent version of the whole text, in Italian and English, see J. P. Richter (1939, **2**, 379).]

[2] 'Caterina arrived on July 16, 1493.'—'Giovannina—a fabulous face—Call on Caterina in the hospital and make enquiries.'

even for him there were occasions when what had been suppressed obtained expression forcibly. The death of the mother he had once loved so dearly was one of these. What we have before us in the account of the costs of the funeral is the expression—distorted out of all recognition—of his mourning for his mother. We wonder how such distortion could come about, and indeed we cannot understand it if we treat it as a normal mental process. But similar processes are well known to us in the abnormal conditions of neurosis and especially of what is known as 'obsessional neurosis'. There we can see how the expression of intense feelings, which have however become unconscious through repression, is displaced on to trivial and even foolish actions. The expression of these repressed feelings has been lowered by the forces opposed to them to such a degree that one would have had to form a most insignificant estimate of their intensity; but the imperative compulsiveness with which this trivial expressive act is performed betrays the real force of the impulses—a force which is rooted in the unconscious and which consciousness would like to deny. Only a comparison such as this with what happens in obsessional neurosis can explain Leonardo's account of the expenses of his mother's funeral. In his unconscious he was still tied to her by erotically coloured feelings, as he had been in childhood. The opposition that came from the subsequent repression of this childhood love did not allow him to set up a different and worthier memorial to her in his diary. But what emerged as a compromise from this neurotic conflict had to be carried out; and thus it was that the account was entered in the diary, and has come to the knowledge of posterity as something unintelligible.

It does not seem a very extravagant step to apply what we have learnt from the funeral account to the reckonings of the pupils' expenses. They would then be another instance of the scanty remnants of Leonardo's libidinal impulses finding expression in a compulsive manner and in a distorted form. On that view, his mother and his pupils, the likeness of his own boyish beauty, had been his sexual objects—so far as the sexual repression which dominated his nature allows us to describe them—and the compulsion to note in laborious detail the sums he spent on them betrayed in this strange way his rudimentary conflicts. From this it would appear that Leonardo's erotic life did really belong to the type of homosexuality whose psychical development we have succeeded in disclosing, and the emergence of the homosexual situation in his phantasy of the vulture would become intelligible to us: for its meaning was exactly what we have already asserted of that type. We should have to translate it thus: 'It was through this erotic relation with my mother that I became a homosexual.'[1]

---

[1] The forms of expression in which Leonardo's repressed libido was allowed to show itself—circumstantiality and concern over money—are among the traits of character which result from anal erotism. See my 'Character and Anal Erotism' (1908b).

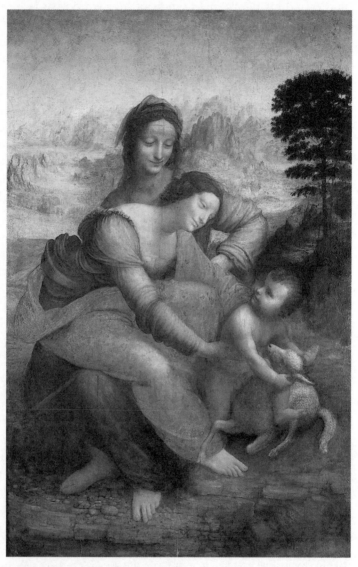

Virgin and Child with St Anne. Vinci, Leonardo da/Louvre, Paris, France/ Giraudon/The Bridgeman Art Library.

4

We have not yet done with Leonardo's vulture phantasy. In words which only too plainly recall a description of a sexual act ('and struck me many times with its tail against[1] my lips'), Leonardo stresses the intensity of the erotic relations between mother and child. From this linking of his mother's (the vulture's) activity with the prominence of the mouth zone it is not difficult to guess that a second memory is contained in the phantasy. This may be translated: 'My mother pressed innumerable passionate kisses on my mouth.' The phantasy is compounded from the memory of being suckled and being kissed by his mother.

Kindly nature has given the artist the ability to express his most secret mental impulses, which are hidden even from himself, by means of the works that he creates; and these works have a powerful effect on others who are strangers to the artist, and who are themselves unaware of the source of their emotion. Can it be that there is nothing in Leonardo's life work to bear witness to what his memory preserved as the strongest impression of his

[1] [See footnote 1, p. 30.]

childhood? One would certainly expect there to be something. Yet if one considers the profound transformations through which an impression in an artist's life has to pass before it is allowed to make its contribution to a work of art, one will be bound to keep any claim to certainty in one's demonstration within very modest limits; and this is especially so in Leonardo's case.

Anyone who thinks of Leonardo's paintings will be reminded of a remarkable smile, at once fascinating and puzzling, which he conjured up on the lips of his female subjects. It is an unchanging smile, on long, curved lips; it has become a mark of his style and the name 'Leonardesque' has been chosen for it.[1] In the strangely beautiful face of the Florentine Mona Lisa del Giocondo it has produced the most powerful and confusing effect on whoever looks at it. [See p. 60.] This smile has called for an interpretation, and it has met with many of the most varied kinds, none of which has been satisfactory. 'Voilà quatre siècles bientôt que Monna Lisa fait perdre la tête à tous ceux qui parlent d'elle, après l'avoir longtemps regardée.'[2]

Muther (1909, 1, 314) writes: 'What especially casts a spell on the spectator is the daemonic magic of this smile. Hundreds of poets and authors have written about this woman who now appears to smile on us so seductively, and now to stare coldly and without soul into space; and no one has solved the riddle of her smile, no one has read the meaning

---

[1] [*Footnote added* 1919:] The connoisseur of art will think here of the peculiar fixed smile found in archaic Greek sculptures—in those, for example, from Aegina; he will perhaps also discover something similar in the figures of Leonardo's teacher Verrocchio and therefore have some misgivings in accepting the arguments that follow.

[2] ['For almost four centuries now Mona Lisa has caused all who talk of her, after having gazed on her for long, to lose their heads.'] The words are Gruyer's, quoted by von Seidlitz (1909, 2, 280).

of her thoughts. Everything, even the landscape, is mysteriously dream-like, and seems to be trembling in a kind of sultry sensuality.'

The idea that two distinct elements are combined in Mona Lisa's smile is one that has struck several critics. They accordingly find in the beautiful Florentine's expresssion the most perfect representation of the contrasts which dominate the erotic life of women; the contrast between reserve and seduction, and between the most devoted tenderness and a sensuality that is ruthlessly demanding—consuming men as if they were alien beings. This is the view of Müntz (1899, 417): 'On sait quelle énigme indéchiffrable et passionnante Monna Lisa Gioconda ne cesse depuis bientôt quatre siècles de proposer aux admirateurs pressés devant elle. Jamais artiste (j'emprunte la plume du délicat écrivain qui se cache sous le pseudonyme de Pierre de Corlay) "a-t-il traduit ainsi l'essence même de la fémininité: tendresse et coquetterie, pudeur et sourde volupté, tout le mystère d'un coeur qui se réserve, d'un cerveau qui réfléchit, d'une personnalité qui se garde et ne livre d'elle-même que son rayonnement . . ."[1] The Italian writer Angelo Conti (1910, 93) saw the picture in the Louvre brought to life by a ray of sunshine. 'La donna sorrideva in una calma regale: i suoi istinti di conquista, di ferocia, tutta l'eredità della specie, la volontá della seduzione e dell' agguato, la grazia del inganno, la bontà che cela un proposito crudele, tutto ciò appariva alternativamente e scompariva dietro il velo ridente e si fondeva nel poema del suo sorriso . . .

---

[1] ['We know what an insoluble and enthralling enigma Mona Lisa Gioconda has never ceased through nearly four centuries to pose to the admirers that throng in front of her. No artist (I borrow the words from the sensitive writer who conceals himself behind the pseudonym of Pierre de Corlay) "has ever expressed so well the very essence of femininity: tenderness and coquetry, modesty and secret sensuous joy, all the mystery of a heart that holds aloof, a brain that meditates, a personality that holds back and yields nothing of itself save its radiance".']

Buona e malvagia, crudele e compassionevole, graziosa e felina, ella rideva . . .'[1]

Leonardo spent four years painting at this picture, perhaps from 1503 to 1507, during his second period of residence in Florence, when he was over fifty. According to Vasari he employed the most elaborate artifices to keep the lady amused during the sittings and to retain the famous smile on her features. In its present condition the picture has preserved but little of all the delicate details which his brush reproduced on the canvas at that time, while it was being painted it was considered to be the highest that art could achieve, but it is certain that Leonardo himself was not satisfied with it, declaring it to be incomplete, and did not deliver it to the person who had commissioned it, but took it to France with him, where his patron, Francis I, acquired it from him for the Louvre.

Let us leave unsolved the riddle of the expression on Mona Lisa's face, and note the indisputable fact that her smile exercised no less powerful a fascination on the artist than on all who have looked at it for the last four hundred years. From that date the captivating smile reappears in all his pictures and in those of his pupils. As Leonardo's Mona Lisa is a portrait, we cannot assume that he added on his own account such an expressive feature to her face—a feature that she did not herself possess. The conclusion seems hardly to be avoided that he found this smile in his model and fell so strongly under its spell that from then on he bestowed it on the free creations of his phantasy. This interpretation, which cannot be called far-fetched, is put forward, for example, by Konstantinowa (1907, 44):

[1] ['The lady smiled in regal calm: her instincts of conquest, of ferocity, all the heredity of the species, the will to seduce and to ensnare, the charm of deceit, the kindness that conceals a cruel purpose,—all this appeared and disappeared by turns behind the laughing veil and buried itself in the poem of her smile . . . Good and wicked, cruel and compassionate, graceful and feline, she laughed . . .']

'During the long period in which the artist was occupied with the portrait of Mona Lisa del Giocondo, he had entered into the subtle details of the features on this lady's face with such sympathetic feeling that he transferred its traits—in particular the mysterious smile and the strange gaze—to all the faces that he painted or drew afterwards. The Gioconda's peculiar facial expression can even be perceived in the picture of John the Baptist in the Louvre; but above all it may be clearly recognized in the expression on Mary's face in the "Madonna and Child with St. Anne".'[1] [See the Frontispiece of this volume.]

Yet this situation may also have come about in another way. The need for a deeper reason behind the attraction of La Gioconda's smile, which so moved the artist that he was never again free of it, has been felt by more than one of his biographers. Walter Pater, who sees in the picture of Mona Lisa a 'presence . . . expressive of what in the ways of a thousand years men had come to desire' [1873, 118], and who writes very sensitively of 'the unfathomable smile, always with a touch of something sinister in it, which plays over all Leonardo's work' [ibid., 117], leads us to another clue when he declares (loc. cit.):

'Besides the picture is a portrait. From childhood we see this image defining itself on the fabric of his dreams; and but for express historical testimony, we might fancy that this was but his ideal lady, embodied and beheld at last . . .'

Marie Herzfeld (1906, 88) has no doubt something very similar in mind when she declares that in the Mona Lisa Leonardo encountered his own self and for this reason was able to put so much of his own nature into the picture 'whose features had lain all along in mysterious sympathy within Leonardo's mind'.

Let us attempt to clarify what is suggested here. It may very well have been that Leonardo was fascinated by Mona Lisa's

---

[1] [The title of this subject in German is 'heilige Anna Selbdritt', literally 'St. Anne with Two Others', a point which is referred to below, p. 67.]

smile for the reason that it awoke something in him which had for long lain dormant in his mind—probably an old memory. This memory was of sufficient importance for him never to get free of it when it had once been aroused; he was continually forced to give it new expression. Pater's confident assertion that we can see, from childhood, a face like Mona Lisa's defining itself on the fabric of his dreams, seems convincing and deserves to be taken literally.

Vasari mentions that 'teste di femmine, che ridono'[1] formed the subject of Leonardo's first artistic endeavours. The passage—which, since it is not intended to prove anything, is quite beyond suspicion—runs more fully according to Schorn's translation (1843, **3**, 6): 'In his youth he made some heads of laughing women out of clay, which were reproduced in plaster, and some children's heads which were as beautiful as if they had been modelled by the hand of a master . . .'

Thus we learn that he began his artistic career by portraying two kinds of objects; and these cannot fail to remind us of the two kinds of sexual objects that we have inferred from the analysis of his vulture-phantasy. If the beautiful children's heads were reproductions of his own person as it was in his childhood, then the smiling women are nothing other than repetitions of his mother Caterina, and we begin to suspect the possibility that it was his mother who possessed the mysterious smile—the smile that he had lost and that fascinated him so much when he found it again in the Florentine lady.[2]

The painting of Leonardo's which stands nearest to the Mona Lisa in point of time is the so-called 'St. Anne with Two Others',

---

[1] ['Heads of laughing women.'] Quoted by Scognamiglio (1900, 32).

[2] The same assumption is made by Merezhkovsky. But the history of Leonardo's childhood as he imagines it departs at the essential points from the conclusions we have drawn from the phantasy of the vulture. Yet if the smile had been that of Leonardo himself [as Merezhkovsky also assumes] tradition would hardly have failed to inform us of the coincidence.

St. Anne with the Madonna and child. [See the Frontispiece.] In it the Leonardesque smile is most beautifully and markedly portrayed on both the women's faces. It is not possible to discover how long before or after the painting of the Mona Lisa Leonardo began to paint this picture. As both works extended over years, it may, I think, be assumed that the artist was engaged on them at the same time. It would best agree with our expectations if it was the intensity of Leonardo's preoccupation with the features of Mona Lisa which stimulated him to create the composition of St. Anne out of his phantasy. For if the Gioconda's smile called up in his mind the memory of his mother, it is easy to understand how it drove him at once to create a glorification of motherhood, and to give back to his mother the smile he had found in the noble lady. We may therefore permit our interest to pass from Mona Lisa's portrait to this other picture—one which is hardly less beautiful, and which to-day also hangs in the Louvre.

St. Anne with her daughter and her grandchild is a subject that is rarely handled in Italian painting. At all events Leonardo's treatment of it differs widely from all other known versions. Muther (1909, **1**, 309) writes:

'Some artists, like Hans Fries, the elder Holbein and Girolamo dai Libri, made Anne sit beside Mary and put the child between them. Others, like Jakob Cornelisz in his Berlin picture, painted what was truly a "St. Anne with Two Others";[1] in other words, they represented her as holding in her arms the small figure of Mary upon which the still smaller figure of the child Christ is sitting.' In Leonardo's picture Mary is sitting on her mother's lap, leaning forward, and is stretching out both arms towards the boy, who is playing with a young lamb and perhaps treating it a little unkindly. The grandmother rests on her hip the arm that is not concealed and gazes down on the pair with a blissful smile.

---

[1] [I.e., St. Anne was the most prominent figure in the picture. See footnote, p. 65 above.]

The grouping is certainly not entirely unconstrained. But although the smile that plays on the lips of the two women is unmistakably the same as that in the picture of Mona Lisa, it has lost its uncanny and mysterious character; what it expresses is inward feeling and quiet blissfulness.[1]

After we have studied this picture for some time, it suddenly dawns on us that only Leonardo could have painted it, just as only he could have created the phantasy of the vulture. The picture contains the synthesis of the history of his childhood: its details are to be explained by reference to the most personal impressions in Leonardo's life. In his father's house he found not only his kind stepmother, Donna Albiera, but also his grandmother, his father's mother, Monna Lucia, who—so we will assume—was no less tender to him than grandmothers usually are. These circumstances might well suggest to him a picture representing childhood watched over by mother and grandmother. Another striking feature of the picture assumes even greater significance. St. Anne, Mary's mother and the boy's grandmother, who must have been a matron, is here portrayed as being perhaps a little more mature and serious than the Virgin Mary, but as still being a young woman of unfaded beauty. In point of fact Leonardo has given the boy two mothers, one who stretches her arms out to him, and another in the background; and both are endowed with the blissful smile of the joy of motherhood. The peculiarity of the picture has not failed to surprise those who have written about it: Muther, for example, is of the opinion that Leonardo could not bring himself to paint old age, lines and wrinkles, and for this reason made Anne too into a woman of radiant beauty. But can we be satisfied with this

---

[1] Konstantinowa (1907, [44]): 'Mary gazes down full of inward feeling on her darling, with a smile that recalls the mysterious expression of La Gioconda.' In another passage [ibid., 52] she says of Mary: 'The Gioconda's smile hovers on her features.'

explanation? Others have had recourse to denying that there is any similarity in age between the mother and daughter.[1] But Muther's attempt at an explanation is surely enough to prove that the impression that St. Anne has been made more youthful derives from the picture and is not an invention for an ulterior purpose.

Leonardo's childhood was remarkable in precisely the same way as this picture. He had had two mothers: first, his true mother Caterina, from whom he was torn away when he was between three and five, and then a young and tender step-mother, his father's wife, Donna Albiera. By his combining this fact about his childhood with the one mentioned above (the presence of his mother and grandmother)[2] and by his condensing them into a composite unity, the design of 'St. Anne with Two Others' took shape for him. The maternal figure that is further away from the boy—the grandmother—corresponds to the earlier and true mother, Caterina, in its appearance and in its special relation to the boy. The artist seems to have used the blissful smile of St. Anne to disavow and to cloak the envy which the unfortunate woman felt when she was forced to give up her son to her better-born rival, as she had once given up his father as well.[3]

---

[1] Von Seidlitz (1909, **2**, 274, notes).

[2] [The words in parentheses were added in 1923.]

[3] [*Footnote added* 1919:] If an attempt is made to separate the figures of Anne and Mary in this picture and to trace the outline of each, it will not be found altogether easy. One is inclined to say that they are fused with each other like badly condensed dream-figures, so that in some places it is hard to say where Anne ends and where Mary begins. But what appears to a critic's eye [in 1919 only: 'to an artist's eye'] as a fault, as a defect in composition, is vindicated in the eyes of analysis by reference to its secret meaning. It seems that for the artist the two mothers of his childhood were melted into a single form.

[*Added* 1923:] It is especially tempting to compare the 'St. Anne with Two Others' of the Louvre with the celebrated London cartoon, where the same

We thus find a confirmation in another of Leonardo's works of our suspicion that the smile of Mona Lisa del Giocondo had awakened in him as a grown man the memory of the mother of

materials is used to form a different composition [See Fig. 2.] Here the forms of the two mothers are fused even more closely and their separate outlines are even harder to make out, so that critics, far removed from any attempt to offer an interpretation, have been forced to say that it seems 'as if two heads were growing from a single body'.

Most authorities are in agreement in pronouncing the London cartoon to be the earlier work and in assigning its origin to Leonardo's first period in Milan (before 1500). Adolf Rosenberg (1898), on the other hand, sees the composition of the cartoon as a later—and more successful—version of the same theme, and follows Anton Springer in dating it even after the Mona Lisa. It would fit in excellently with our arguments if the cartoon were to be much the earlier work. It is also not hard to imagine how the picture in the Louvre arose out of the cartoon, while the reverse course of events would make no sense. If we take the composition shown in the cartoon as our starting point, we can see how Leonardo may have felt the need to undo the dream-like fusion of the two women—a fusion corresponding to his childhood memory—and to separate the two heads in space. This came about as follows: From the group formed by the mothers he detached Mary's head and the upper part of her body and bent them downwards. To provide a reason for this displacement the child Christ had to come down from her lap on to the ground. There was then no room for the little St. John, who was replaced by the lamb.

[*Added* 1919:] A remarkable discovery has been made in the Louvre picture by Oskar Pfister, which is of undeniable interest, even if one may not feel inclined to accept it without reserve. In Mary's curiously arranged and rather confusing drapery he has discovered the *outline of a vulture* and he interprets it as an *unconscious picture puzzle:*—

'In the picture that represents the artist's mother *the vulture, the symbol of mother-hood,* is perfectly clearly visible.

'In the length of blue cloth, which is visible around the hip of the woman in front and which extends in the direction of her lap and her right knee, one can see the vulture's extremely characteristic head, its neck and the sharp curve where its body begins. Hardly any observer whom I have confronted with my little find has been able to resist the evidence of this picture-puzzle.' (Pfister, 1913, 147.).

At this point the reader will not, I feel sure, grudge the effort of looking at

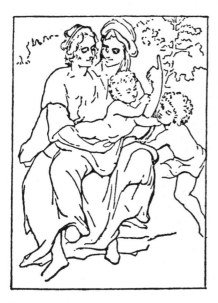

Figure 2

his earliest childhood. From that time onward, madonnas and aristocratic ladies were depicted in Italian painting humbly bowing their heads and smiling the strange, blissful smile of Caterina, the poor peasant girl who had brought into the world

the accompanying illustration, to see if he can find in it the outlines of the vulture seen by Pfister. The piece of blue cloth, whose border marks the edges of the picture-puzzle, stands out in the reproduction as a light grey field against the darker ground of the rest of the drapery. [See the Frontispiece and Fig. 3.]

Pfister continues: 'The important question however is: How far does the picture-puzzle extend? If we follow the length of cloth, which stands out so sharply from its surroundings, starting at the middle of the wing and continuing from there, we notice that one part of it runs down to the woman's foot, while the other part extends in an upward direction and rests on her shoulder and on the child. The former of these parts might more or less represent the vulture's wing and tail, as it is in nature; the latter might be a pointed belly and—especially when we notice the radiating lines which resemble the

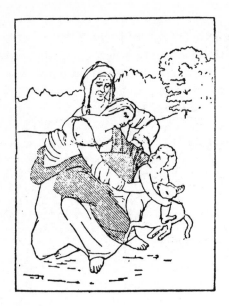

Figure 3

the splendid son who was destined to paint, to search and to suffer.

If Leonardo was successful in reproducing on Mona Lisa's face the double meaning which this smile contained, the promise of unbounded tenderness and at the same time sinister menace (to quote Pater's phrase [above, p. 65]), then here too he had remained true to the content of his earliest memory. For his mother's tenderness was fateful for him; it determined his destiny and the privations that were in store for him. The violence of the caresses, to which his phantasy of the vulture points, was

outlines of feathers— a bird's outspread tail, whose right-hand end, *exactly as in Leonardo's fateful childhood dream* [sic], *leads to the mouth of the child, i.e. of Leonardo himself.*'

The author goes on to examine the interpretation in greater detail, and discusses the difficulties to which it gives rise.

only too natural. In her love for her child the poor forsaken mother had to give vent to all her memories of the caresses she had enjoyed as well as her longing for new ones; and she was forced to do so not only to compensate herself for having no husband, but also to compensate her child for having no father to fondle him. So, like all unsatisfied mothers, she took her little son in place of her husband, and by the too early maturing of his erotism robbed him of a part of his masculinity. A mother's love for the infant she suckles and cares for is something far more profound than her later affection for the growing child. It is in the nature of a completely satisfying love-relation, which not only fulfils every mental wish but also every physical need; and if it represents one of the forms of attainable human happiness, that is in no little measure due to the possibility it offers of satisfying, without reproach, wishful impulses which have long been repressed and which must be called perverse.[1] In the happiest young marriage the father is aware that the baby, especially if he is a baby son, has become his rival, and this is the starting-point of an antagonism towards the favourite which is deeply rooted in the unconscious.

When, in the prime of life, Leonardo once more encountered the smile of bliss and rapture which had once played on his mother's lips as she fondled him, he had for long been under the dominance of an inhibition which forbade him ever again to desire such caresses from the lips of women. But he had become a painter, and therefore he strove to reproduce the smile with his brush, giving it to all his pictures (whether he in fact executed them himself or had them done by his pupils under his direction)—to Leda, to John the Baptist and to Bacchus. The last two are variants of the same type. 'Leonardo has turned the locust-eater of the Bible', says Muther [1909, 1, 314], 'into a Bacchus, a young Apollo, who, with a mysterious smile on his

---

[1] See my *Three Essays on the Theory of Sexuality* (1905d), [*Standard Ed.*, 7, 233].

lips, and with his smooth legs crossed, gazes at us with eyes that intoxicate the senses.' These pictures breathe a mystical air into whose secret one dares not penetrate; at the very most one can attempt to establish their connection with Leonardo's earlier creations. The figures are still androgynous, but no longer in the sense of the vulture-phantasy. They are beautiful youths of feminine delicacy and with effeminate forms; they do not cast their eyes down, but gaze in mysterious triumph, as if they knew of a great achievement of happiness, about which silence must be kept. The familiar smile of fascination leads one to guess that it is a secret of love. It is possible that in these figures Leonardo has denied the unhappiness of his erotic life and has triumphed over it in his art, by representing the wishes of the boy, infatuated with his mother, as fulfilled in this blissful union of the male and female natures.

5

Among the entries in Leonardo's notebooks there is one which catches the reader's attention owing to the importance of what it contains and to a minute formal error.

In July 1504 he writes:

'Adi 9 di Luglio 1504 mercoledi a ore 7 mori Ser Piero da Vinci, notalio al palazzo del Potestà, mio padre, a ore 7. Era d'età d'anni 80, lasciò 10 figlioli maschi e 2 femmine.'[1]

As we see, the note refers to the death of Leonardo's father. The small error in its form consists of the repetition of the time of day 'a ore 7' [at 7 o'clock], which is given twice, as if Leonardo had forgotten at the end of the sentence that he had already written it at the beginning. It is only a small detail, and anyone who was not a psycho-analyst would attach no importance to it. He might not even notice it, and if his attention was drawn to it he might say that a thing like that can happen to anyone in a moment of distraction or of strong feeling, and that it has no further significance.

---

[1] ['On July 9, 1504, Wednesday at 7 o'clock died Ser Piero da Vinci, notary at the palace of the Podestà, my father, at 7 o'clock. He was 80 years old, and left 10 sons and 2 daughters.'] After Müntz (1899, 13n).

The psycho-analyst thinks differently. To him nothing is too small to be a manifestation of hidden mental processes. He has learnt long ago that such cases of forgetting or repetition are significant, and that it is the 'distraction' which allows impulses that are otherwise hidden to be revealed.

We would say that this note, like the account for Caterina's funeral [pp. 56–7] and the bills of the pupils' expenses [pp. 55–6], is a case in which Leonardo was unsuccessful in suppressing his affect and in which something that had long been concealed forcibly obtained a distorted expression. Even the form is similar: there is the same pedantic exactness, and the same prominence given to numbers.[1]

We call a repetition of this kind a perseveration. It is an excellent means of indicating affective colour. One recalls, for example, St. Peter's tirade in Dante's *Paradiso* against his unworthy representative on earth:

> Quegli ch'usurpa in terra il luogo mio,
> Il luogo mio, il luogo mio, che vaca
> Nella presenza del Figliuol di Dio,
>
> Fatto ha del cimiterio mio cloaca.[2]

With Leonardo's affective inhibition the entry in his diary might have run somewhat as follows: 'To-day at 7 o'clock my father died—Ser Piero da Vinci, my poor father!' But the displacement of the perseveration on to the most indifferent detail in the report of his death, the hour at which he died, robs the entry of

---

[1] I am leaving on one side a greater error made by Leonardo in this note by giving his father's age as 80 instead of 77. [See also note 1 on page 77.]

[2] ['He who usurps on earth my place, my place, my place, which in the presence of the Son of God is vacant, has made a sewer of the ground where I am buried.'] Canto XXVII, 22–25.

all emotion, and further lets us see that here was something to be concealed and suppressed.

Ser Piero da Vinci, notary and descendant of notaries, was a man of great energy who reached a position of esteem and prosperity. He was married four times. His first two wives died childless, and it was only his third wife who presented him with his legitimate son, in 1476, by which time Leonardo had reached the age of 24 and had long ago exchanged his father's home for the studio of his master Verrochio. By his fourth and last wife, whom he married when he was already in his fifties, he had nine more sons and two daughters.[1]

It cannot be doubted that his father too came to play an important part in Leonardo's psychosexual development, and not only negatively by his absence during the boy's first childhood years, but also directly by his presence in the later part of Leonardo's childhood. No one who as a child desires his mother can escape wanting to put himself in his father's place, can fail to identify himself with him in his imagination, and later to make it his task in life to gain ascendancy over him. When Leonardo was received into his grandfather's house before he had reached the age of five, his young step-mother Albiera must certainly have taken his mother's place where his feelings were concerned, and he must have found himself in what may be called the normal relationship of rivalry with his father. As we know, a decision in favour of homosexuality only takes place round about the years of puberty. When this decision had been arrived at in Leonardo's case, his identification with his father lost all significance for his sexual life, but it nevertheless continued in other spheres of non-erotic activity. We hear that he was fond of magnificence and fine clothes, and kept servants and horses,

---

[1] Leonardo has apparently made a further mistake in this passage in his diary over the number of his brothers and sisters—a remarkable contrast to the apparent exactness of the passage.

although, in Vasari's words, 'he possessed almost nothing and did little work'. The responsibility for these tastes is not to be attributed solely to his feeling for beauty: we recognize in them at the same time a compulsion to copy and to outdo his father. His father had been a great gentleman to the poor peasant girl, and the son, therefore, never ceased to feel the spur to play the great gentleman as well, the urge 'to out-herod Herod',[1] to show his father what a great gentleman really looks like.

There is no doubt that the creative artist feels towards his works like a father. The effect which Leonardo's identification with his father had on his paintings was a fateful one. He created them and then cared no more about them, just as his father had not cared about him. His father's later concern could change nothing in this compulsion; for the compulsion derived from the impressions of the first years of childhood, and what has been repressed and has remained unconscious cannot be corrected by later experiences.

In the days of the Renaissance—and even much later—every artist stood in need of a gentleman of rank, a benefactor and patron, who gave him commissions and in whose hands his fortune rested. Leonardo found his patron in Lodovico Sforza, called Il Moro, a man of ambition and a lover of splendour, astute in diplomacy, but of erratic and unreliable character. At his court in Milan Leonardo passed the most brilliant period of his life, and in his service his creative power attained its most uninhibited expansion, to which the Last Supper and the equestrian statue of Francesco Sforza bore witness. He left Milan before catastrophe overtook Lodovico Sforza, who died a prisoner in a French dungeon. When the news of his patron's fate reached Leonardo, he wrote in his diary: 'The duke lost his dukedom and his property and his liberty, and none of the

---

[1] [The last three words are in English in the original.]

works that he undertook was completed.'[1] It is remarkable, and certainly not without significance, that he here cast the same reproach at his patron which posterity was to bring against himself. It is as if he wanted to make someone from the class of his fathers responsible for the fact that he himself left his works unfinished. In point of fact he was not wrong in what he said about the duke.

But if his imitation of his father did him damage as an artist, his rebellion against his father was the infantile determinant of what was perhaps an equally sublime achievement in the field of scientific research. In Merezhkovsky's admirable simile (1903, 348), he was like a man who had awoken too early in the darkness, while everyone else was still asleep. He dared to utter the bold assertion which contains within itself the justification for all independent research: '*He who appeals to authority when there is a difference of opinion works with his memory rather than with his reason.*'[2] Thus he became the first modern natural scientist, and an abundance of discoveries and suggestive ideas rewarded his courage for being the first man since the time of the Greeks to probe the secrets of nature while relying solely on observation and his own judgement. But in teaching that authority should be looked down on and that imitation of the 'ancients' should be repudiated, and in constantly urging that the study of nature was the source of all truth, he was merely repeating—in the highest sublimation attainable by man—the one-sided point of view which had already forced itself on the little boy as he gazed in wonder on the world. If we translate scientific abstraction back again into concrete individual experience, we see that the 'ancients' and authority simply correspond to his father, and

---

[1] 'Il duca perse lo stato e la roba e libertà e nessuna sua opera si finì per lui.' Quoted by Von Seidlitz (1909, **2**, 270).

[2] 'Chi disputa allegando l'autorità non adopra l'ingegno ma piuttosto la memoria.' Quoted by Solmi (1910, 13). [Codex Atlanticus, F. 76r.a.]

nature once more becomes the tender and kindly mother who had nourished him. In most other human beings—no less today than in primaeval times—the need for support from an authority of some sort is so compelling that their world begins to totter if that authority is threatened. Only Leonardo could dispense with that support; he would not have been able to do so had he not learnt in the first years of his life to do without his father. His later scientific research, with all its boldness and independence, presupposed the existence of infantile sexual researches uninhibited by his father, and was a prolongation of them with the sexual element excluded.

When anyone has, like Leonardo, escaped being intimidated by his father during his earliest[1] childhood, and has in his researches cast away the fetters of authority, it would be in the sharpest contradiction to our expectation if we found that he had remained a believer and had been unable to escape from dogmatic religion. Psycho-analysis has made us familiar with the intimate connection between the father-complex and belief in God; it has shown us that a personal God is, psychologically, nothing other than an exalted father, and it brings us evidence every day of how young people lose their religious beliefs as soon as their father's authority breaks down. Thus we recognize that the roots of the need for religion are in the parental complex; the almighty and just God, and kindly Nature, appear to us as grand sublimations of father and mother, or rather as revivals and restorations of the young child's ideas of them. Biologically speaking, religiousness is to be traced to the small human child's long-drawn-out helplessness and need of help; and when at a later date he perceives how truly forlorn and weak he is when confronted with the great forces of life, he feels his condition as he did in childhood, and attempts to deny his own despondency by a regressive revival of the forces which protected his infancy.

[1] [This word was added in 1925.]

The protection against neurotic illness, which religion vouch-safes to those who believe in it, is easily explained: it removes their parental complex, on which the sense of guilt in individuals as well as in the whole human race depends, and disposes of it, while the unbeliever has to grapple with the problem on his own.[1]

It does not seem as if the instance of Leonardo could show this view of religious belief to be mistaken. Accusations charging him with unbelief or (what at that time came to the same thing) with apostasy from Christianity were brought against him while he was still alive, and are clearly described in the first biography which Vasari [1550] wrote of him. (Müntz, 1899, 299 ff.) In the second (1568) edition of his *Vite* Vasari omitted these observations. In view of the extraordinary sensitiveness of his age where religious matters were in question, we can understand perfectly why even in his notebooks Leonardo should have refrained from directly stating his attitude to Christianity. In his researches he did not allow himself to be led astray in the slightest degree by the account of the Creation in Holy Writ; he challenged, for example, the possibility of a universal Deluge, and in geology he calculated in terms of hundreds of thousands of years with no more hesitation than men in modern times.

Among his 'prophecies' there are some things that would have been bound to offend the sensitive feelings of a Christian believer. Take for example, 'On the practice of praying to the images of saints':

'Men will speak to men that perceive nothing, that have their eyes open and see nothing; they will talk to them and receive no answer; they will implore the grace of those that have ears and

---

[1] This last sentence was added in 1919.—The same point is mentioned in Freud's contemporary address to the Nuremberg Congress (1910d), and again, much later, in the last chapter of *Group Psychology* (1921c), *Standard Ed.*, **18**, 142.]

hear not; they will kindle lights for one that is blind.' (After Herzfeld, 1906, 292.).

Or 'On the mourning on Good Friday':

'In every part of Europe great peoples will weep for the death of a single man who died in the East.' (Ibid., 297.).

The view has been expressed about Leonardo's art that he took from the sacred figures the last remnant of their connection with the Church and made them human, so as to represent by their means great and beautiful human emotions. Muther praises him for overcoming the prevailing mood of decadence and for restoring to man his right to sensuality and the joy of living. In the notes that show Leonardo engrossed in fathoming the great riddles of nature there is no lack of passages where he expresses his admiration for the Creator, the ultimate cause of all these noble secrets; but there is nothing which indicates that he wished to maintain any personal relation with this divine power. The reflections in which he has recorded the deep wisdom of his last years of life breathe the resignation of the human being who subjects himself to' Ανάγκη, to the laws of nature, and who expects no alleviation from the goodness or grace of God. There is scarcely any doubt that Leonardo had prevailed over both dogmatic and personal religion, and had by his work of research removed himself far from the position from which the Christian believer surveys the world.

The findings, mentioned above [p. 44 ff], which we have reached concerning the development of the mental life of children suggest the view that in Leonardo's case too the first researches of childhood were concerned with the problems of sexuality. Indeed he himself gives this away in a transparent disguise by connecting his urge for research with the vulture phantasy, and by singling out the problem of the flight of birds as one to which, as the result of a special chain of circumstances, he was destined to turn his attention. A highly obscure passage in his notes which is concerned with the flight of birds, and which sounds like a prophecy, gives a very good demonstration of the degree of affective interest with which he clung to his wish to succeed in imitating the art of flying himself:'The great bird will take its first flight from the back of its Great Swan; it will fill the universe with stupefaction, and all writings with renown, and be the eternal glory of the nest where it was born.'[1] He probably hoped that he himself would be able to fly one day, and we know from wish-fulfilling dreams what bliss is expected from the fulfilment of that hope.

But why do so many people dream of being able to fly? The answer that psycho-analysis gives is that to fly or to be a bird is only a disguise for another wish, and that more than one bridge, involving words or things, leads us to recognize what it is. When we consider that inquisitive children are told that babies are brought by a large bird, such as the stork; when we find that the ancients represented the phallus as having wings; that the commonest expression in German for male sexual activity is '*vögeln*' ['to bird': '*Vogel*' is the German for 'bird']; that the male organ is actually called '*l'uccello*' ['the bird'] in Italian—all of these are only small fragments from a whole mass of connected ideas, from which we learn that in dreams the wish to be able to fly is to be understood as nothing else than a longing to be capable of sexual performance.[2] This is an early infantile wish. When an adult recalls his childhood it seems to him to have been a happy time, in which one enjoyed the moment and looked to the future without any wishes; it is for this reason that he envies children. But if children themselves were able to give us

---

[1] After Herzfeld (1906, 32). 'The Great Swan' seems to mean Monte Cecero, a hill near Florence [now Monte Ceceri: '*Cecero*' is Italian for 'swan'].

[2] [*Footnote added* 1919:] This statement is based on the researches of Paul Federn [1914] and of Mourly Vold (1912), a Norwegian man of science who had no contact with psycho-analysis. [See also *The Interpretation of Dreams* (1900*a*), *Standard Ed.*, **5**, 394.]

information earlier[1] they would probably tell a different story. It seems that childhood is not the blissful idyll into which we distort it in retrospect, and that, on the contrary, children are goaded on through the years of childhood by the one wish to get big and do what grown-ups do. This wish is the motive of all their games. Whenever children feel in the course of their sexual researches that in the province which is so mysterious but nevertheless so important there is something wonderful of which adults are capable but which they are forbidden to know of and do, they are filled with a violent wish to be able to do it, and they dream of it in the form of flying, or they prepare this disguise of their wish to be used in their later flying dreams. Thus aviation, too, which in our day is at last achieving its aim, has its infantile erotic roots.

In admitting to us that ever since his childhood he felt bound up in a special and personal way with the problem of flight, Leonardo gives us confirmation that his childhood researches were directed to sexual matters; and this is what we were bound to expect as a result of our investigations on children in our own time. Here was one problem at least which had escaped the repression that later estranged him from sexuality. With slight changes in meaning, the same subject continued to interest him from his years of childhood until the time of his most complete intellectual maturity; and it may very well be that the skill that he desired was no more attainable by him in its primary sexual sense than in its mechanical one, and that he remained frustrated in both wishes.

Indeed, the great Leonardo remained like a child for the whole of his life in more than one way; it is said that all great men are bound to retain some infantile part. Even as an adult he continued to play, and this was another reason why he often appeared uncanny and incomprehensible to his contempories. It

---

[1] ['Früher.' In the editions before 1923 'darüber' appears in place of 'früher', giving the meaning 'about it'.]

is only we who are unsatisfied that he should have constructed the most elaborate mechanical toys for court festivities and ceremonial receptions, for we are reluctant to see the artist turning his power to such trifles. He himself seems to have shown no unwillingness to spend his time thus, for Vasari tells us that he made similar things when he had not been commissioned to do so: 'There (in Rome) he got a soft lump of wax, and made very delicate animals out of it, filled with air; when he blew into them they flew around, and when the air ran out they fell to the ground. For a peculiar lizard which was found by the wine-grower of Belvedere he made wings from skin torn from other lizards, and filled them with quicksilver, so that they moved and quivered when it walked. Next he made eyes, a beard and horns for it, tamed it and put it in a box and terrified all his friends with it.'[1] Such ingenuities often served to express thoughts of a serious kind. 'He often had a sheep's intestines cleaned so carefully that they could have been held in the hollow of the hand. He carried them into a large room, took a pair of blacksmith's bellows into an adjoining room, fastened the intestines to them and blew them up, until they took up the whole room and forced people to take refuge in a corner. In this way he showed how they gradually became transparent and filled with air; and from the fact that at first they were limited to a small space and gradually spread through the whole breadth of the room, he compared them to genius.'[2] The same playful delight in harmlessly concealing things and giving them ingenious disguises is illustrated by his fables and riddles. The latter are cast into the form of 'prophecies': almost all are rich in ideas and to a striking degree devoid of any element of wit.

The games and pranks which Leonardo allowed his imagination have in some cases led his biographers, who

[1] Vasari, from Schorn's translation (1843, 39) [ed. Poggi, 1919, 41].

[2] Ibid., 39 [ed. Poggi, 41].

misunderstood this side of his character, grievously astray. In Leonardo's Milanese manuscripts there are, for example, some drafts of letters to the 'Diodario of Sorio (Syria), Viceroy of the Holy Sultan of Babylonia', in which Leonardo presents himself as an engineer sent to those regions of the East to construct certain works; defends himself against the charge of laziness; supplies geographical descriptions of towns and mountains, and concludes with an account of a great natural phenomenon that occurred while he was there.[1]

In 1883 an attempt was made by J. P. Richter to prove from these documents that it was really a fact that Leonardo had made these observations while travelling in the service of the Sultan of Egypt, and had even adopted the Mohammedan religion when in the East. On this view his visit there took place in the period before 1483—that is, before he took up residence at the court of the Duke of Milan. But the acumen of other authors has had no difficulty in recognizing the evidences of Leonardo's supposed Eastern journey for what they are—imaginary productions of the youthful artist, which he created for his own amusement and in which he may have found expression for a wish to see the world and meet with adventures.

Another probable example of a creation of his imagination is to be found in the 'Academia Vinciana' which has been postulated from the existence of five or six emblems, intertwined patterns of extreme intricacy, which contain the Academy's name. Vasari mentions these designs but not the Academy.[2]

---

[1] For these letters and the various questions connected with them see Müntz (1899, 82 ff.); the actual texts and other related notes will be found in Herzfeld (1906, 223 ff.).

[2] 'Besides, he lost some time by even making a drawing of knots of cords, in which it was possible to trace the thread from one end to the other until it formed a completely circular figure. A very complex and beautiful design of this sort is engraved on copper; in the middle can be read the words "Leonardus Vinci Academia".' Schorn (1843, 8) [ed. Poggi, 5].

Müntz, who put one of these ornaments on the cover of his large work on Leonardo, is among the few who believe in the reality of an 'Academia Vinciana'.

It is probable that Leonardo's play-instinct vanished in his maturer years, and that it too found its way into the activity of research which represented the latest and highest expansion of his personality. But its long duration can teach us how slowly anyone tears himself from his childhood if in his childhood days he has enjoyed the highest erotic bliss, which is never again attained.

6

It would be futile to blind ourselves to the fact that readers to-day find all pathography unpalatable. They clothe their aversion in the complaint that a pathographical review of a great man never results in an understanding of his importance and his achievements, and that it is therefore a piece of useless impertinence to make a study of things in him that could just as easily be found in the first person one came across. But this criticism is so manifestly unjust that it is only understandable when taken as a pretext and a disguise. Pathography does not in the least aim at making the great man's achievements intelligible; and surely no one should be blamed for not carrying out something he has never promised to do. The real motives for the opposition are different. We can discover them if we bear in mind that biographers are fixated on their heroes in a quite special way. In many cases they have chosen their hero as the subject of their studies because—for reasons of their personal emotional life—they have felt a special affection for him from the very first. They then devote their energies to a task of idealization, aimed at enrolling the great man among the class of their infantile models—at reviving in him, perhaps, the child's idea of his father. To gratify this wish they obliterate the individual features of their subject's physiognomy; they smooth over the traces of his life's struggles with internal and external resistances, and they tolerate in him no vestige of human weakness or imperfection. They thus present us with what is in fact a cold, strange, ideal figure, instead of a human being to whom we might feel ourselves distantly related. That they should do this is regrettable, for they thereby sacrifice truth to an illusion, and for the sake of their infantile phantasies abandon the opportunity of penetrating the most fascinating secrets of human nature.[1]

Leonardo himself, with his love of truth and his thirst for knowledge, would not have discouraged an attempt to take the trivial peculiarities and riddles in his nature as a starting-point, for discovering what determined his mental and intellectual development. We do homage to him by learning from him. It does not detract from his greatness if we make a study of the sacrifices which his development from childhood must have entailed, and if we bring together the factors which have stamped him with the tragic mark of failure.

We must expressly insist that we have never reckoned Leonardo as a neurotic or a 'nerve case', as the awkward phrase goes. Anyone who protests at our so much as daring to examine him in the light of discoveries gained in the field of pathology is still clinging to prejudices which we have to-day rightly abandoned. We no longer think that health and illness, normal and neurotic people, are to be sharply distinguished from each other, and that neurotic traits must necessarily be taken as proofs of a general inferiority. To-day we know that neurotic symptoms are structures which are substitutes for certain achievements of repression that we have to carry out in the course of our development from a child to a civilized human being. We know too that we all

---

[1] This criticism applies quite generally and is not to be taken as being aimed at Leonardo's biographers in particular.

produce such substitutive structures, and that it is only their number, intensity and distribution which justify us in using the practical concept of illness and in inferring the presence of constitutional inferiority. From the slight indications we have about Leonardo's personality we should be inclined to place him close to the type of neurotic that we describe as 'obsessional'; and we may compare his researches to the 'obsessive brooding' of neurotics, and his inhibitions to what are known as their 'abulias'.

The aim of our work has been to explain the inhibitions in Leonardo's sexual life and in his artistic activity. With this in view we may be allowed to summarize what we have been able to discover about the course of his physical development.

We have no information about the circumstances of his heredity; on the other hand we have seen that the accidental conditions of his childhood had a profound and disturbing effect on him. His illegitimate birth deprived him of his father's influence until perhaps his fifth year, and left him open to the tender seductions of a mother whose only solace he was. After being kissed by her into precocious sexual maturity, he must no doubt have embarked on a phase of infantile sexual activity of which only one single manifestation is definitely attested—the intensity of his infantile sexual researches. The instinct to look and the instinct to know were those most strongly excited by the impressions of his childhood; the erotogenic zone of the mouth was given an emphasis which it never afterwards surrendered. From his later behaviour in the contrary direction, such as his exaggerated sympathy for animals, we can conclude that there was no lack of strong sadistic traits in this period of his childhood.

A powerful wave of repression brought this childhood excess to an end, and established the dispositions which were to become manifest in the years of puberty. The most obvious result of the transformation was the avoidance of every crudely sensual activity; Leonardo was enabled to live in abstinence and to give the impression of being an asexual human being. When the excitations of puberty came in their flood upon the boy they did not, however, make him ill by forcing him to develop substitutive structures of a costly and harmful kind. Owing to his very early inclination towards sexual curiosity the greater portion of the needs of his sexual instinct could be sublimated into a general urge to know, and thus evaded repression. A much smaller portion of his libido continued to be devoted to sexual aims and represented a stunted adult sexual life. Because his love for his mother had been repressed, this portion was driven to take up a homosexual attitude and manifested itself in ideal love for boys. The fixation on his mother and on the blissful memories of his relations with her continued to be preserved in the unconscious, but for the time being it remained in an inactive state. In this way repression, fixation and sublimation all played their part in disposing of the contributions which the sexual instinct made to Leonardo's mental life.

Leonardo emerges from the obscurity of his boyhood as an artist, a painter and a sculptor, owing to a specific talent which may have been reinforced by the precocious awakening in the first years of childhood of his scopophilic instinct. We should be most glad to give an account of the way in which artistic activity derives from the primal instincts of the mind if it were not just here that our capacities fail us. We must be content to emphasize the fact—which it is hardly any longer possible to doubt—that what an artist creates provides at the same time an outlet for his sexual desire; and in Leonardo's case we can point to the information which comes from Vasari [above, p. 66], that heads of laughing women and beautiful boys—in other words, representations of his sexual objects—were notable among his first artistic endeavours. In the bloom of his youth Leonardo appears at first to have worked without inhibition. Just as he modelled himself on his father in the outward conduct of his life, so too he passed through a period of masculine creative power and artistic productiveness in Milan, where a kindly fate enabled him to find a father-substitute in the duke Lodovico Moro. But soon we find confirmation of our experience that the almost total repression of a real sexual life does not provide the most favourable conditions for the exercise of sublimated sexual trends. The pattern imposed by sexual life made itself felt. His activity and his ability to form quick decisions began to fail; his tendency towards deliberation and delay was already noticeable as a disturbing element in the 'Last Supper', and by influencing his technique it had a decisive effect on the fate of that great painting. Slowly there occurred in him a process which can only be compared to the regressions in neurotics. The development that turned him into an artist at puberty was overtaken by the process which led him to be an investigator, and which had its determinants in early infancy. The second sublimation of his erotic instinct gave place to the original sublimation for which the way had been prepared on the occasion of the first repression. He became an investigator, at first still in the service of his art, but later independently of it and away from it. With the loss of his patron, the substitute for his father, and with the increasingly sombre colours which his life took on, this regressive shift assumed larger and larger proportions. He became 'impacientissimo al pennello',[1] as we are told by a correspondent of the Countess Isabella d'Este, who was extremely eager to possess a painting from his hand. His infantile past had gained control over him. But the research which now took the place of artistic creation seems to have contained some of the features which distinguish the activity of unconscious instincts—insatiability, unyielding rigidity and the lack of an ability to adapt to real circumstances.

At the summit of his life, when he was in his early fifties—a time when in women the sexual characters have already undergone involution and when in men the libido not infrequently

---

[1] ['Very impatient of painting.'] Von Seidlitz (1909, **2**, 271).

makes a further energetic advance—a new transformation came over him. Still deeper layers of the contents of his mind became active once more; but this further regression was to the benefit of his art, which was in the process of becoming stunted. He met the woman who awakened his memory of his mother's happy smile of sensual rapture; and, influenced by this revived memory, he recovered the stimulus that guided him at the beginning of his artistic endeavours, at the time when he modelled the smiling women. He painted the Mona Lisa, the 'St. Anne with Two Others' and the series of mysterious pictures which are characterized by the enigmatic smile. With the help of the oldest of all his erotic impulses he enjoyed the triumph of once more conquering the inhibition in his art. This final development is obscured from our eyes in the shadows of approaching age. Before this his intellect had soared upwards to the highest realizations of a conception of the world that left his epoch far behind it.

In the preceding chapters I have shown what justification can be found for giving this picture of Leonardo's course of development—for proposing these subdivisions of his life and for explaining his vacillation between art and science in this way. If in making these statements I have provoked the criticism, even from friends of psycho-analysis and from those who are expert in it, that I have merely written a psycho-analytic novel, I shall reply that I am far from over-estimating the certainty of these results. Like others I have succumbed to the attraction of this great and mysterious man, in whose nature one seems to detect powerful instinctual passions which can nevertheless only express themselves in so remarkably subdued a manner.

But whatever the truth about Leonardo's life may be, we cannot desist from our endeavour to find a psycho-analytic explanation for it until we have completed another task. We must stake out in a quite general way the limits which are set to what psycho-analysis can achieve in the field of biography: otherwise every explanation that is not forthcoming will be held up to us as a failure. The material at the disposal of a psycho-analytic enquiry consists of the data of a person's life history: on the one hand the chance circumstances of events and background influences, and, on the other hand, the subject's reported reactions. Supported by its knowledge of psychical mechanisms it then endeavours to establish a dynamic basis for his nature on the strength of his reactions, and to disclose the original motive forces of his mind, as well as their later transformations and developments. If this is successful the behaviour of a personality in the course of his life is explained in terms of the combined operation of constitution and fate, of internal forces and external powers. Where such an undertaking does not provide any certain results—and this is perhaps so in Leonardo's case—the blame rests not with the faulty or inadequate methods of psycho-analysis, but with the uncertainty and fragmentary nature of the material relating to him which tradition makes available. It is therefore only the author who is to be held responsible for the failure, by having forced psycho-analysis to pronounce an expert opinion on the basis of such insufficient material.

But even if the historical material at our disposal were very abundant, and if the psychical mechanisms could be dealt with with the greatest assurance, there are two important points at which a psycho-analytic enquiry would not be able to make us understand how inevitable it was that the person concerned should have turned out in the way he did and in no other way. In Leonardo's case we have had to maintain the view that the accident of his illegitimate birth and the excessive tenderness of his mother had the most decisive influence on the formation of his character and on his later fortune, since the sexual repression which set in after this phase of childhood caused him to sublimate his libido into the urge to know, and established his sexual inactivity for the whole of his later life. But this repression after the first erotic satisfactions of childhood need not necessarily have taken place; in someone else it might perhaps not have taken place or might have assumed much less extensive proportions. We must recognize here a degree of freedom which cannot be resolved any further by psycho-analytic means. Equally, one has no right to claim that the consequence of this wave of repression was the only possible one. It is probable that another person would not have succeeded in withdrawing the major portion of his libido from repression by sublimating it into a craving for knowledge; under the same influences he would have sustained a permanent injury to his intellectual activity or have acquired an insurmountable disposition to obsessional neurosis. We are left, then, with these two characteristics of Leonardo which are inexplicable by the efforts of psycho-analysis: his quite special tendency towards instinctual repressions, and his extraordinary capacity for sublimating the primitive instincts.

Instincts and their transformations are at the limit of what is discernible by psycho-analysis. From that point it gives place to biological research. We are obliged to look for the source of the tendency to repression and the capacity for sublimation in the organic foundations of character on which the mental structure is only afterwards erected. Since artistic talent and capacity are intimately connected with sublimation we must admit that the nature of the artistic function is also inaccessible to us along psycho-analytic lines. The tendency of biological research to-day is to explain the chief features in a person's organic constitution as being the result of the blending of male and female dispositions, based on [chemical] substances. Leonardo's physical beauty and his left-handedness might be quoted in support of this view.[1] We will not, however, leave the ground of purely

[1] [This is no doubt an allusion to the views of Fliess by which Freud had been greatly influenced. Cf. his *Three Essays* (1905d), *Standard Ed.*, **7**, 216n. On the particular question of bilaterality, however, they had not been in complete agreement. See above, p. 4n.]

psychological research. Our aim remains that of demonstrating the connection along the path of instinctual activity between a person's external experiences and his reactions. Even if psychoanalysis does not throw light on the fact of Leonardo's artistic power, it at least renders its manifestations and its limitations intelligible to us. It seems at any rate as if only a man who had had Leonardo's childhood experiences could have painted the Mona Lisa and the St. Anne, have secured so melancholy a fate for his works and have embarked on such an astonishing career as a natural scientist, as if the key to all his achievements and misfortunes lay hidden in the childhood phantasy of the vulture.

But may one not take objection to the findings of an enquiry which ascribes to accidental circumstances of his parental constellation so decisive an influence on a person's fate—which, for example, makes Leonardo's fate depend on his illegitimate birth and on the barrenness of his first stepmother Donna Albiera? I think one has no right to do so. If one considers chance to be unworthy of determining our fate, it is simply a relapse into the pious view of the Universe which Leonardo himself was on the way to overcoming when he wrote that the sun does not move [p. 23]. We naturally feel hurt that a just God and a kindly providence do not protect us better from such influences during the most defenceless period of our lives. At the same time we are all too ready to forget that in fact everything to do with our life is chance, from our origin out of the meeting of spermatozoon and ovum onwards—chance which nevertheless has a share in the law and necessity of nature, and which merely lacks any connection with our wishes and illusions. The apportioning of the determining factors of our life between the 'necessities' of our constitution and the 'chances' of our childhood may still be uncertain in detail; but in general it is no longer possible to doubt the importance precisely of the first years of our childhood. We all still show too little respect for Nature which (in the obscure words of Leonardo which recall Hamlet's lines) 'is full of countless causes ['*ragioni*'] that never enter experience'.[1]

Every one of us human beings corresponds to one of the countless experiments in which these '*ragioni*' of nature force their way into experience.

---

[1] '*La natura è piena d'infinite ragioni che non furono mai in isperienza*' (Herzfeld, 1906, 11).—[The allusion seems to be to Hamlet's familiar words:

There are more things in heaven and earth, Horatio,
Than are dreamt of in your philosophy.]

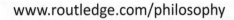

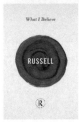

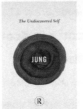

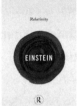

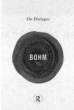

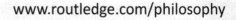

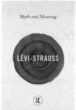

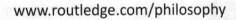
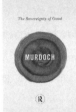